LONDON IN YOUR POCKET

Judy Wachs

LONDON IN YOUR POCKET

A handy directory of restaurants, hotels, museums, theaters, stores, nightlife, famous landmarks—the best of the city's sights, services, and pleasures!

Second Edition

Woodbury, New York • London • Toronto Sydney

Credits

Underground map courtesy of London Transport Executive.
Central London and Around London maps courtesy of British Tourist Authority.

Illustrations by Juan Suarez.

Book design by Milton Glaser, Inc.

Inclusion of a particular store or service in this guide should not be construed as a recommendation from the Publisher. All noted sources and services subject to change; we suggest that you phone ahead.

© Copyright 1985 by Barron's Educational Series, Inc.
Prior edition © Copyright 1982
by Barron's Educational Series, Inc.

All rights reserved.
No part of this book may be reproduced
in any form, by photostat, microfilm,
xerography, or any other means, or
incorporated into any information
retrieval system, electronic or
mechanical, without the written
permission of the copyright owner.

All inquiries should be addressed to:
Barron's Educational Series, Inc.
113 Crossways Park Drive
Woodbury, New York 11797

Library of Congress Catalog Card No. 84-21614

International Standard Book No. 0-8120-2973-9

Library of Congress Cataloging in Publication Data
Main entry under title:

London in your pocket.

  1. London (England)–Description–1981– –Guidebooks. I. Barron's Educational Series, inc.
DA679.L824   1985   914.21′204858   84-21614
ISBN 0-8120-2973-9

PRINTED IN THE UNITED STATES OF AMERICA

567   880   987654321

CONTENTS

Preface	7
Finding Your Way Around Town	9
Annual Events	11
Antiques	15
Art Galleries	17
Art Supplies	19
Auction Houses	20
Bakeries and Pastry Shops	21
Bicycle Rentals	23
Books About London	23
Bookstores	24
Boutiques	27
Cheese Shops	29
Children's London	30
Chocolate and Candy	36
Coffee and Tea	37
Department Stores	37
Drugstores	40
Excursions Out of London	40
Fabric Shops	42
Gay Scene	43

Haberdasheries	49
Hospital and Health Emergencies	50
Hotels	51
Information	64
Jewelry Shops	66
Leather Goods	68
Limousines	68
Markets	69
Movie Theaters	72
Museums	73
Music, Opera and Dance	81
Musical Instruments	82
Newspapers and Magazines	83
Nightlife	84
Parks	88
Perfumes and Toiletries	91
Pubs	92
Records and Tapes	95
Restaurants	97
Royal London	123
Sights Worth Seeing	127
Singles Clubs	134
Sports and Sporting Events	135

Contents

Theater	**139**
Tours and Sightseeing	**144**
Toys	**145**
Transportation	**146**
Weather	**147**
Wine Bars	**148**
Wines and Liquors	**149**

Maps	**151**
Central London	**152**
Around London	**156**
Tips for Taking the Underground	**158**
London Underground	inside back cover
London and Environs	inside front cover

PREFACE

"When a man is tired of London, he is tired of life; for there is in London all that life can afford."

Dr. Johnson said it more than 200 years ago, but it's still true—perhaps even more so now, as the pressures of urban development, crime and decay make so many other great cities around the world less pleasant than they used to be. London has traffic jams too, of course, but unlike the drivers in most other European cities, the people in them rarely honk their horns, and so the atmosphere remains peaceful. When two Londoners collide on a crowded sidewalk, they both instinctively apologize ("sorry," "sorry"), and there is none of the abuse and recrimination that you would expect in Paris or New York.

To both the newcomer and the native, this wonderfully civil city still offers "all that life can afford," and this book can help you find it. Strangers may at first be puzzled by the constant reference to postal codes—W1, EC2, and such. The reason is that they are an essential part of an address, even when there is clearly no thought of mailing a letter. Few streets in London are more than a few blocks long, and many of them have the same name. There are, for example, 59 different streets, roads, and alleyways in London named "Gloucester"; you'll need a zone number to know which is which.

Besides the maps in this book, the newcomer to London should buy the paperback *A–Z* (pronounced "A-to-Zed") map book, for exploring the city. Most tourists will do far better with the large-scale "Inner London" version than with the citywide *A–Z*, which covers a greater area but is much harder to read. Both are published by Geographers' A–Z Map Company, and are available at newsstands and bookstores.

This book can be a help in planning your assault on London. But most of the real joys of the place are serendipitous: suddenly coming upon a resplendent mounted unit of the Queen's guard on a frosty morning in Hyde Park, the sun gleaming on their swords and helmets; finding just the right little shop selling the very best of just exactly whatever-it-is-you're-looking-for, with a kindly proprietor who seems to have walked straight out of the pages of Dickens; meeting the typical aging cockney woman who calls you "love," in the very first sentence she utters, and promises to "make you a nice cup of tea," the solution to every problem. Unless you're "tired of life," you can find it all in London.

ACKNOWLEDGMENTS

We gratefully acknowledge the help of William Borders of the New York *Times*, London Bureau, in researching and preparing the material for the first edition. We thank Lindsay Fairgrieve for helping prepare this second edition.

FINDING YOUR WAY AROUND TOWN

Because London is such an ancient city, many of its streets twist and wind confusingly (following what used to be a cow path or a horse trail). And just to make it harder, they also change their names every few blocks, reflecting a history that goes back to the days when it was a major excursion to cover a few miles. As a result, many residents could not begin to tell you the names of all the streets even in their own neighborhood. But getting lost here is part of the fun.

The City of London is the old square mile around St. Paul's Cathedral and the Tower. It's called "The City," and when Londoners use that term, they are referring only to that neighborhood; nothing else. The City is where most of the banks and other financial institutions are situated, and so the term is used, as the term "Wall Street" is, to mean "the financial community," as in the sentence, "The City reacted with hostility to the budget proposals."

To the west of The City is Westminster, which includes most of the principal tourist attractions, and west and south of that lies the Royal Borough of Kensington and Chelsea. Though joined administratively now, Kensington and Chelsea are still thought of as two distinct geographical entities, both largely residential and generally quite fashionable. The legendary King's Road—which is still good for people-watching, especially on Saturdays—runs through the middle of Chelsea.

Around Town

LORD NELSON STATUE IN TRAFALGAR SQUARE

ANNUAL EVENTS

January

Perhaps because it is so bleak and wintry, January has become the month for huge and wondrous exhibitions at which you can enter another world for the afternoon. Olympia Stadium, Hammersmith Road, W14, has a camping and outdoor life exhibition, followed by the international holiday exhibition and then a show of racing cars. There is the annual boat show at the Earl's Court Exhibition Building (behind the Earl's Court tube station), where you can climb aboard some of the very grandest yachts, and the model engineering exhibition at Seymour Hall, Seymour Place, W1.

February

The Chinese New Year (sometimes earlier) brings dancing to the streets of the Chinese Quarter of Soho. At the Cruft's Dog Show, Olympia, you can see the legendary affection between the Englishman and his dog. At the Crystal Palace Sports Centre, SE19, there is a national canoe exhibition.

March

The Daily Mail Ideal Home Exhibition, Olympia, lasts most of March, and is very popular with homemakers. At the Crystal Palace, there is an exhibition of dinghies. The storied boat race between the crews of Oxford and Cambridge takes place in March or sometimes April; it goes on the Thames, from Putney to Mortlake. Usually there is a royal film performance, in which a new movie is attended by royalty in aid of charity, an occasion of much glitter and flash.

April

Easter Sunday (sometimes in March, of course) is a big day in London, with church services and hymn programs in a number of splendid places. The carol service in Westminster Abbey on Easter Monday (the day after Easter; a holiday in Britain) is memorable. On Easter Sunday there is a vibrant carnival procession in Battersea Park SW11 (south of the river), and there are also fairs at Wormwood Scrubs, Hampstead Heath, and Blackheath. On Maundy Thursday, the Thursday before Easter, Queen Elizabeth presents Maundy money to pensioners. Her birthday is April 21, and although it is officially celebrated in the summer (when the weather is usually better), she gets a 21-gun salute on the day itself. The Greater London Festival—with pageants, art shows, and carnivals—usually begins in late April.

May

By May, London has put the long winter behind and outdoor events begin in earnest. The Beating Retreat, a spectacular royal ceremony in which the Queen is featured on horseback, is the highlight of the month. It takes place in Horseguards Parade, just east of St. James's Park. The Chelsea Flower Show, in the Royal Hospital Grounds, SW3, is another welcome sign of spring. The Football Association Cup Final at Wembley, a suburb, is the climax of the British football season (comparable to the baseball World Series in the United States), usually the first Saturday in May. The London fire brigades have a competition of target water spraying (sometimes in June) in Guildhall Yard, EC2. On the third or fourth Saturday is the London to Brighton Walk, which started in 1903. And there are also the National Sheep Dog trials in Hyde Park, open-air art exhibitions in Victoria Embankment Gardens, WC2, and amateur regattas on the Thames at Putney and Hammersmith. Starting on May 31–June 8 is the Fine Arts and Antiques Fair at Olympia.

June

The world's foremost tennis championship at Wimbledon, a suburb south of the Thames, begins the last week of June. Even if you do not go there, catch a bit of it on television! The tournament is given blanket coverage, especially by BBC 2. Election of the Sheriffs of the City of London (the central historical core of the city, now the financial district) has the Lord Mayor and the aldermen in a colorful ceremony. The 600-year-old Garter Ceremony at St. George's Chapel, Windsor (outside London; see EXCURSIONS), includes a colorful procession of the Household Cavalry and the Yeomen of the Guard. The Henley Regatta is at Henley-on-Thames outside London (sometimes July). Trooping the Color, another bit of rich royal pageantry, is the Queen's procession from Buckingham Palace down the Mall to Horseguards Parade and back. Marching bands, horses, troops—all the wondrous show that the world loves and the British royal family does so well.

July

City of London music festival, held every other year, includes splendid concerts of choral and orchestral music, in St. Paul's Cathedral and Mansion House. Royal International Horse Show, Wembley, features first-rate show jumping, and since the Royal family are fond of horses, they are usually well represented in the audience. Royal Tournament, Earl's Court, is a marvelously impressive military spectacle, with marching bands and massed brass bands. A must for anyone who loves band music. The Sunday before it opens, which is usually in the middle of July, the bands stage a colorful parade in Battersea Park.

August

The August Bank Holiday weekend, at the end of the month, is comparable to Labor Day weekend in the United States, marking the end of summer, and there are many outdoor events during it, including a fair in Hampstead Heath and a horse show in Clapham Common, SW4. August 4 is the birthday of the much-beloved Queen Mother, which means she gets a gun salute.

September

Battle of Britain Week salutes the heroes of that battle with a Royal Air Force flypast over Westminster on the 15th, and a memorial service in Westminster

Annual Events

Abbey the following Sunday. The Chelsea Antiques Fair in the Old Town Hall, Chelsea SW3, attracts a lot of attention. Gillette Cup Finals in Cricket, at Lord's Cricket Grounds, St. John's Wood, NW8.

October

Thanksgiving service for the Harvest of the Sea at St. Mary at Hill, Lovat Lane EC3. The fish sellers from the historic old Billingsgate Market decorate the church with fish nets. Horse of the Year show at Wembley, show jumping. The international motor show at Earl's Court, very popular. At the Royal Albert Hall, a brass band festival, with some of the best in Britain.

November

The admission of the new Lord Mayor of London (a ceremonial job) is the occasion for a colorful procession through the old part of town, from Mansion House to Guildhall, with fireworks afterwards over the river (second Saturday). To mark Armistice Day, there is a very moving ceremony at the Cenotaph in Whitehall (second Sunday). November 5 is Guy Fawkes Day, the anniversary of the gunpowder plot of 1605, and there are displays of fireworks all over the country. At Earl's Court, in the middle of the month, an exhibition of trailers and camping equipment. The State Opening of Parliament, usually early in the month, is another of those glittering royal occasions, with the Queen and her family riding from Buckingham Palace to the House of Lords in the Irish State coach, as a salute is fired in St. James's Park. For car buffs, there is the vintage automobile race from London to Brighton, starting from Hyde Park Corner. It celebrates the day in 1896 when the speed limit was raised from 4 miles per hour.

December

Christmastime in London, no matter how dreary the weather, always seems exciting. The choicest shopping areas—Regent Street, Mayfair and Knightsbridge—are alive with colored lights and luxurious window displays. Each year the people of Norway send a huge tree which is erected in Trafalgar Square, and

Annual Events

Christmas carols are played at the base. There is Christmas music all over town, from stately Westminster Abbey to the little parish church.

ANTIQUES

Most of the finest antique shops in London are in Mayfair or in the Fulham Road/King's Road area. What follows is only a selection of some of the best. As usual, in the business of antiquing, you are most likely to find something that appeals to you by wandering. Most shops open at 9 or 9:30 every day but Sunday. Some open on Saturdays only by appointment.

Antique Porcelain Company 149 New Bond Street, W1; 629-1254. Eighteenth-century English & Continental porcelain, French furniture, gold boxes and Renaissance jewels.

Antiquarius Antique Market 135–141 King's Road, SW3; 351-5353. A wide selection of art deco, Victorian nighties, furniture, jewelry.

Aptel Fredericks 265–267 Fulham Road, SW3; 352-2188. Furniture from late 17th- to early 19th-centuries. William & Mary to early Regency.

Barling of Mount Street 112 Mount Street, W1; 499-2858. Specializes in Chinese and Japanese works of art and European 16th- and 17th-century oak furniture.

Fernandes & Marche 23 Motcomb Street, SW1; 235-0601. Specializes in mirrors and console tables; English 18th-century.

Harriet Wynter 50 Redcliffe Road, SW10; 352-6494. Antique instruments such as telescopes and navigational aids.

Hotspur 14 Lowndes Street, SW1; 235-1918. Absolutely top quality, with prices to match. Sells to museums, but it is a wonderful place to visit even if you can't afford it.

How of Edinburgh 2 Pickering Place, St. James's Street, SW1; 930-7140. Early English and Scottish silver, in a picturesque, 250-year-old house that is itself an interesting antique.

J. Crotty & Son 74 New King's Road, SW6; 731-4209. Specializes in fireplace equipment: screens, pokers, and elegant little shovels.

Jeremy 255 King's Road, SW3; 352-0644. A stylish shop with first-rate 18th-century English and French furniture and objects d'art.

John Keil 154 Brompton Road, SW3; 589-6454. This shop has English 18th-century furniture of outstanding quality.

John Sparks 128 Mount Street, W1; 499-2265. One of London's leading shops for Oriental art, pottery, lacquer furniture, early Chinese bronzes.

Jonathan Potter Ltd. 1 Grafton Street, W1; 491-3520. Antique maps, prints and altases.

Mallet & Son (Antiques) Ltd. 40 New Bond Street, W1; 499-7411. Enormous and famous shop full of 18th-century furniture. Anyone interested in antiques must have a look at Mallet.

Naxos Art Ltd. 27 Mount Street, W1; 629-6448. Specialists in Roman, Greek and Islamic antiquities.

Norman Adams 8–10 Hans Road, SW3; 589-5266. A small shop on basement and ground floor, opposite Harrods, with some outstanding 18th-century English furniture.

Partridge 144–146 New Bond Street, W1; 629-0834. A beautiful shop, with the very finest French and English silver and furniture.

Portmeirion Antiques 62 Whitehart Lane, Barnes, SW13; 876-2367. Two floors of Victoriana and a large stock of English and Continental furniture, china pictures and other decorative details.

Richard Courtney 112–114 Fulham Road, SW3; 370-4020. Eighteenth-century furniture and works of art.

Alistair Sampson Antiques 156 Brompton Road, SW3; 589-5272. Pottery, brass, English Delft plates, primitive paintings, English oak furniture, plaques, urns and needlework.

Simon Kaye 18 Dover Street, W1; 493-7658. Antique silver dating back to Elizabethan times, as well as Victorian and old Sheffield plate.

S. J. Phillips 139 New Bond Street, W1; 629-6261. Absolutely first-rate antique English and Continental silver.

Shrubsole 43 Museum Street, WC1; 405-2712. A wonderful collection of antique silver and old Sheffield plate.

Stair & Company 120 Mount Street, W1; 499-1784. Very good selection of 18th-century English furniture. Barometers, chandeliers, mirrors and some Regency objets d'art.

William Redford 9 Mount Street, W1; 629-1165. Continental European furniture and works of art. Interesting shop.

See also AUCTION HOUSES.

ART GALLERIES

Some of the finest art in the world is bought and sold in London. And if you are only interested in looking at it, that's okay too. These are some of the best shops. Most are open from 9:30 or 10 in the morning until 5 or 6, including Saturdays. You'll see that many of them are in Mayfair, W1, which is still the center of the business. But good shops are scattered all over the rest of town as well.

Agnew's 43 Old Bond Street, W1; 629-6176. Some of the best paintings in a number of fields, including Old Masters and English watercolors and French and English drawings.

Angela Flowers 11–12 Tottenham Mews, W1; 637-3089. A showcase for new talent about to reach the top.

Anneley Juda 11 Tottenham Mews, W1; 637-5517. Contemporary painting and sculpture; Russian constructivism.

Baskett & Day 173 New Bond Street, W1; 629-2991. Especially good for Old Master and English drawings and paintings.

Browse and Darby 19 Cork Street, W1; 734-7984. Paintings, drawings and sculpture from the 19th- and 20th-centuries.

Colnaghi's 14 Old Bond Street, W1; 491-7408. Top-quality Old Masters and Modern paintings and drawings.

Crane Kalman 178 Brompton Road, SW3; 584-7566. Graham Sutherland, Ben Nicholson, and others.

D'Offay 9 Dering Street, W1; 629-1578. Contemporary English paintings and drawings.

Drian 7 Porchester Place, W2; 723-9473. Scores of artists from various countries. An interesting variety.

Fine Art Society Ltd. 148 New Bond Street, W1; 629-5116. Victorian and Edwardian painting and sculpture.

Fischer Fine Art 30 King Street, SW1; 839-3942. German expressionists, Russian constructivists; also such artists as Ben Jonson, John Ridgewell, and D. H. Smith. Figurative 19th- and 20th-century works from all over Europe.

Francis Kyle 9 Maddox Street, W1; 499-6870. Contemporary watercolors, drawings, etchings, and prints. Some stupendous sculptures.

Gimpel Fils 30 Davies Street, W1; 493-2488. Highly respected gallery with such artists as Larry Rivers and Pierre Soulages. Also, Eskimo sculpture and painting.

Hazlitt, Gooden & Fox 38 Bury Street, SW1; 930-6422. French and English 18th- and 19th-century paintings and drawings. Old Master drawings.

Heim 59 Jermyn Street, SW1; 493-0688. Old Master paintings and sculptures from France and Italy.

Knoedler 22 Cork Street, W1; 439-1096. Contemporary American painters as well as British painters such as Caro and Hockney.

Lefevre 30 Bruton Street, W1; 493-1572. The best in French Impressionists.

Leggatt 17 Duke Street, St. James's, SW1; 930-3772. Wonderful assortment of English pictures covering the last four centuries.

Maas 15A Clifford Street, W1; 734-2302. Victorian paintings, watercolors and drawings.

Marlborough Fine Art 6 Albemarle Street, W1; 629-5161. Some of the best of the contemporary artists, including Graham Sutherland, Franz Kline, Francis Bacon and John Piper.

Mayor 22A Cork Street, W1; 734-3558. Has a number of American artists, including Andy Warhol and Roy Lichtenstein.

New Art Centre 41 Sloane Street, SW1; 235-5844. Twentieth-century British painting.

Nicola Jacobs 9 Cork Street, W1; 437-3868. A new gallery specializing in younger painters.

Art

Nigel Greenwood 41 Sloane Gardens, SW1; 730-8824. Avant-garde gallery with interesting new artists.
Piccadilly 16 Cork Street, W1; 629-2875. Symbolist and contemporary figurative artists.
Portal 16A Grafton Street, W1; 493-0706. Specialists for 25 years in fantasy, self-taught and idiosyncratic painting now recognized as the "Portal School."
Redfern 20 Cork Street, W1; 734-1732. Well-known British and other European painters and sculptors.
Sullivan (Fine Art) 291 New King's Road, SW6; 736-9132. Drawings, watercolors, pictures and sculptures by artists working between 1910–1950. Mainly British.
Treadwell 36 Chiltern Street, W1; 486-1414. Fantasy, erotica and humorous art.
Tryon &Moorland 23–24 Cork Street, W1; 734-6961. Sporting and natural history pictures, prints, bronzes and books.
Waddington 2,4,11,31, & 34 Cork Street, W1; 439-1866. Broad range of contemporary British art.
Wildenstein 147 New Bond Street, W1; 629-0602. Renowned firm with international reputation for excellence.

ART SUPPLIES

Alec Tiranti 21 Goodge Place, W1; 636-8565. Good selection of materials for sculptors and wood carvers.
Felt and Hessian Shop 34 Greville Street, EC1; 405-6215. A good selection of materials for making toys.
Fulham Pottery 184 New King's Road, SW6; 731-2167. Everything for the potter.
Hobby Horse 387 King Street, W6; 748-9636. A big store, with all different kinds of supplies for artists.
J. Blundell & Sons 199 Wardour Street, W1; 437-4746. Marvelous assortment of jewelry bits and costumery.
Paperchase 213 Tottenham Court Road, W1; 580-8496. Every kind of artists' papers.
Winsor & Newton 51–52 Rathbone Place, W1; 636-4231. A wide selection of all kinds of artists' materials.

AUCTION HOUSES

Since London is still arguably the center of the world art market, auction sales are a standard feature of the place. You can bid on anything from a $5 million painting to a $5 antique toy. Upcoming auctions are listed in the *Daily Telegraph* every Monday. Here are the leading houses:

Bonham's Montpelier Galleries Montpelier Street, SW7; 584-9161. Best known for pictures, including even the odd Old Masters, but they also sell carpets, silver, books, and furniture.

Bonham's Chelsea Galleries 65–89 Lots Road, SW10; 352-0466. Bonham's secondary gallery offers the same diversity as its namesake above, specializing in furniture, art and ceramics. Its popularity is probably due to its informal atmosphere and affordable prices.

Christie's 8 King Street, SW1; 839-9060. One of the world's great auction houses, with sales of some of the finest art.

Christie's South Kensington 85 Old Brompton Road, SW7; 581-2231. A much less grand sister establishment selling things that are not up to the world class of Christie's King Street. Someone who just wants to watch might find a more interesting variety here.

Glendining 7 Blenheim Street, W1; 493-2445. An auction house for coins and military and naval medals, in the same premises as Phillips.

Harveys 14–18 Neal Street, WC2; 240-1464. Lower-priced antiques and general furniture.

Marylebone Auction Rooms Hayes Place, NW1; 723-2647. This is where the Phillips house sells furnishings, bric-a-brac, and odd furniture. Good bargains sometimes.

Persian Carpet Galleries 152 Brompton Road, SW3; 584-5516. Auctioneer for antique oriental rugs, with customers all over the world.

Phillips 7 Blenheim Street, W1; 629-6602. London's third-largest auction house (after Sotheby's and Christie's), Phillips covers the same broad range, selling every kind of work of art of the very highest quality.

Phillips West Two 10 Salem Road, W2; 221-5303. Antique and reproduction furniture and porcelain.

Auctions

Sotheby Park Bernet 34–5 New Bond Street, W1; 493-8080. The world's oldest and largest art auctioneers, selling the very best of everything.
Sotheby's Belgravia 19 Motcomb Street, SW1; 235-4311. A branch of Sotheby's selling nothing but Victoriana, art nouveau, and art deco. Pictures, furniture, silver, porcelain.

BAKERIES AND PASTRY SHOPS

Beaton 134 King's Road, SW3; 589-6263. Croissants, scones, and very good fresh bread.
Cranks 8 Marshall Street, W1; 437-2915. Basically a health food shop, Cranks has some of the best bread in London; wheat, fruit breads, cakes and savories. One whiff of the place and you're a customer.
Dugdale and Adams 3 Gerrard Street, W1; 437-3864. Marvelous loaves of French bread.
Maison Verion 12 Bute Street, SW7; 584-0485. Excellent French pastries, catering to the French community that lives in this area.
Paris Croissant 369 Oxford Street, W1; 493-2284. Located next to Bond Street tube, this wonderfully smelling shop lures you to buy highly delectable take-away hot chocolate, apple and apricot croissants and other savories.

BARS
See PUBS, WINE BARS.

HAMPTON COURT

BICYCLE RENTALS

Beta Bikes 275 West End Lane, NW6; 794-4133.
Bicycle Revival 17–19 Elizabeth Street, SW1; 730-6716.
Covent Garden Cycles 37–41 Shorts Gardens, WC2; 836-1752.
Rent-a-Bike Kensington Student Center, Kensington Church Street, W8; 836-7870.
Saviles 97 Battersea Rise, SW11; 228-4279.

BOOKS ABOUT LONDON

There are many, many books about London, some sumptuous, some historical, some worthless. In the shops (see BOOKSTORES), you will find whole sections on this city, good for poring over. The short list that follows, all paperbacks, are books that are useful to the visitor.
Blue Guide Thorough, authoritative, and detailed. Tells you just exactly when and how everything was built, painted, or created. Good maps too.
Egon Ronay's Lucas Guide An annual guide to hotels and restaurants all over the British Isles. Invaluable.
Fodor's London A good general overview of the city, especially for the tourist.
London Shopping Guide by Elsie Burch Donald Penguin paperback. An absolutely exhaustive guide to shopping for anything and everything. Very thorough, very reliable.
Nicholson's Guides Slim little pocket guides to various aspects of London, including nightlife, children's London, restaurant guide, shopping, etc.

Penguin Guide to London by F. R. Banks Gives an in-depth guide to hotels, restaurants, museums, parks, transport, shopping, entertainment and practically everything else there is to know about the history of London.

BOOKSTORES

General and Specialty

London has hundreds of bookshops, and puttering through them is one of the joys of the city. These lists, general and antiquarian, are only a selection, a starting point. Most of the recommended shops have friendly, bookish managers or owners who love chatting about matters literary, and many of them seem to prefer the talk to the actual commerce. Charing Cross Road is the center of the retail book business in London, and many fine shops are on or near it.

Aviation Bookshop 656 Holloway Road, N19; 272-3630. New and secondhand books on every aspect of flight, including space travel.

Bookboat Cutty Sark Gardens, King William Walk, Greenwich, SE10; 853-4383. London's only floating bookshop, the Bookboat is permanently moored at the dock in Greenwich. Specializes in children's books, and they love it.

Books from India Ltd. 45 Museum Street, WC1; 405-7226. A wide selection not only of books, but also pamphlets, catalogs, and information sheets about India and the rest of the subcontinent.

Children's Book Center 229 Kensington High Street, W8; 937-0362. One of the best of the children's bookstores, with books arranged by age, and even a toy department.

Dance Books Ltd. 9 Cecil Court, WC2; 836-2314. An example of the kind of wonderful specialty book shop in which London abounds. Has books about every aspect of dance, from classical ballet to rock and roll.

Dillon's University Bookshop 1 Malet Street, WC1; 636-1577. In the middle of the University of London neighborhood, Dillon's is one of London's premier general bookstores, with titles in every conceivable field, from the erudite classics to the latest trashy novel. The staff is helpful and friendly. Well worth a visit.

Edward Stanford 12–14 Long Acre, WC2; 836-1321. One of the world's largest retail mapsellers for more than a century, Stanford's also has travel books and guides to hiking and other outdoor activities.

Foyle's 119–125 Charing Cross Road, WC1; 437-5660. Foyle's is recommended with some reluctance. It cannot be overlooked because it is by far the largest bookstore in London, and one of the largest in the world. But though the books are there, it is often impossible to find them because of the chaotic way they are organized. And the staff is frequently rude or unhelpful. Too bad, with all those wonderful books to sell.

French's Theater Bookshop 26 Southampton Street, WC2; 836-7513. A delightful old place near the new Covent Garden Market. It stocks books about all aspects of the theater, as well as the texts of plays.

G. Heywood Hill 10 Curzon Street, W1; 629-0647. An enormously pleasant shop, with a wide selection and a staff of people who are delighted to help you find just the right book, new or secondhand.

Hatchards 187 Piccadilly, W1; 439-9921. One of the city's major general bookstores, with a huge selection of all kinds of titles, and a particularly good children's section.

History Bookshop 2 The Broadway, Friern Barnet Road, N11; 368-8568. A considerable distance out of town, but worth the trip if you are a history buff, particularly if the interest is military history. There are also titles on transportation, and a whole section on Winston Churchill.

(J. A. Allen & Co.) The Horseman's Bookshop 1 Lower Grosvenor Place, SW1; 834-5605. Allen's is the leading shop for people interested in horses, and it is appropriately situated just across from the back side of Buckingham Palace.

Motor Books 33 & 36 St. Martin's Court, WC2; 836-5376. Books on cars, trains, and steam vehicles, as well as military and aviation.

Paperchase 213 Tottenham Court Road, W1; 580-8496. Also at 167 Fulham Road, SW3; 589-7839. A wide variety of all kinds of titles, including an especially good children's section.

Pleasures of Past Times 11 Cecil Court, WC2; 836-1142. A picturesque shop featuring secondhand books for children and books on the performing arts and show business. Also has a good collection of Victorian and Edwardian postcards.

Solosy 14, 50 & 53 Charing Cross Road, WC2; 836-6313. General newsdealers also selling books, specializing in the army and navy and military subjects.

Vermillion Books 57 Red Lion Street, WC1; 242-5822. A general bookshop with a good range of titles. It is particularly strong on show business.

Zwemmer's 24 Litchfield Street, WC2; 836-4710. One of the best dealers in books relating to the fine arts.

USED AND ANTIQUARIAN

In addition to the shops listed below, Harrod's is also renowned for its out-of-print book stock.

Bell, Book & Radmall 4 Cecil Court, WC2; 240-2161. This shop claims to have the largest selection in Europe of modern English and American first editions (from the last 100 years).

Bernard Quaritch 5 Lower John Street, W1; 734-2983. Founded in 1847 by Bernard Quaritch, this store is in the same grand old tradition as Maggs (see below). Unlike Maggs, however, it is more difficult to browse in, since many of the books are out of sight.

Bertram Rota 30 Long Acre, WC2; 836-0723. An elegant and friendly shop with a large selection of antiquarian books and first editions. There are also a few new titles, on the subject of modern literature.

Bloomsbury Rare Books 29 Museum Street, WC1; 636-8206. A wide variety of secondhand books, some of them rare and valuable and some of them merely secondhand. There is a good assortment of out-of-print Penguins.

Charles Sawyer 1 Grafton Street, W1; 493-3810. Very rare and expensive books, amid a collection that also includes a good many books by and about Churchill.

Chelsea Rare Books 313 King's Road, SW3; 351-0950. Has a particularly good selection in literature, early travel accounts, and London history books.

Fisher & Speer 46 Highgate High Street, N6; 340-7244. A charming 17th-century building on four floors in the pleasant suburb of Highgate; this large roomy shop has a particularly good selection in literature and topography. There is also a large annex.

Francis Edwards 48A Charing Cross Road, WC2; 379-7669. Specialists in naval and military books.

Green Knight Bookshop 34 St. Martin's Court, WC2; 836-3800. A wonderful old store that specializes in the 19th century, of which it seems itself to be a part.

Henry Sotheran 2–5 Sackville Street, W1; 743-1150. Charles Dickens shopped here. A big selection of secondhand books in every price range, from the very top to the very bottom. Friendly, welcoming atmosphere.

Maggs Bros. 50 Berkeley Square, W1; 499-2007. A wonderful, family-run shop in a 5-story building that is itself a treasure. Maggs is one of the last of the really serious antiquarian booksellers, steeped in a rich London tradition. Despite its wealth of rare books, it has a homey, friendly atmosphere, and its staff obviously knows—and loves—their books.

Otto Haas 49 Belsize Park Gardens, NW3; 722-1488. One of the best stocks on musical literature, autographs and music found in the world.

Pickering & Chatto 17 Pall Mall, SW1; 930-2515. Specialists in travel, economics, medical and science as well as rare antiquarian books.

BOUTIQUES

Boutiques, by which we mean trendy and popular shops for women's clothing and accessories, seem to go in and out of business (and fashion) even more rapidly than most establishments. But what follows is a list of some places currently enjoying success.

Bastet 239 King's Road, SW3; 352-1889. Very brightly colored clothes, strictly for the young and trendy.

Benetton 23 Brompton Road, SW3; 589-6503. A very large selection of separates and Italian knitwear.

Belville-Sassoon 73 Pavilion Road, SW1; 235-5801. English couture. Belinda Belville's own designs—top quality, top price. Also some ready-to-wear.

Browns 23–27 South Molton Street, W1; 499-5630. Stylish separates in an expensive and elegant shop. The best English designers, plus imports.

Che Guevara 44 Kensington High Street, W8; 937-3137. An exciting range of leading designers, colorful jewelry and shoes.

Chic of Hampstead 82 Heath Street, NW3; 435-5454. Very elegant shop, oddly placed in this northern, though fashionable, village. Top British designers and others.

Crocodile 55–7 Beauchamp Place, SW3; 589-1369. One of the most popular boutiques on this very popular street (which, incidentally, is pronounced Beecham Place).

Elle 92 New Bond Street, W1; 629-4441. Clothes which are often featured in *Harper's* and *Vogue*. Expensive English, French and Italian fashions by top designers.

Feathers 40 Hans Crescent, SW1; 589-4621. French and Italian imports. Chiffons, knits, belts and bags.

Frederick Fox 169 Sloane Street, SW1; 235-5618. One of the world's great hat shops.

Fenwicks 63 New Bond Street, W1; 629-9161. A wide selection of various kinds of clothes and accessories.

Jackie O 178 Walton Street, SW3. Elegant leatherware and Italian clothes.

Joseph 6 Sloane Street, SW1; 245-9139. Top-price clothes by top Italian, French and English designers.

Kensington Market 49 Kensington High Street, W8. A sort of supermarket of women's clothes on 3 floors. Wide variety of styles and prices. Especially popular with the young.

Laura Ashley 79 Harriet Street, SW1; 235-9797. Amazingly cheap, very distinctively patterned and romantically styled skirts, nighties and dresses.

Lucienne Phillips 89 Knightsbridge, SW1; 235-2134. Very popular and very expensive. One of the best boutiques in town, some say.

Parkers 31 Brook Street, W1; 493-3412. Small, elegant, expensive.

Boutiques

Piero de Monzi 68–70 Fulham Road, SW3; 581-4247. Immaculate knitwear with sporty clothes from Italy. Expensive.
Regamus 17 Beauchamp Place, SW3; 584-7295. Beautiful day and evening wear in exotic designs.
17 Maiden Lane 17 Maiden Lane, WC2; 379-7889. Wide selection of jeans; sporty and young clothes from well-known designers.
Top Shop Oxford Circus, W1; 636-7700. A huge basement (under Peter Robinson) with a wide selection of new fashions.
Warehouse 202 Earl's Court Road, SW5; 373-2346. Cut-rate, but still stylish clothes.
Way In Harrods, Knightsbridge, SW1; 730-1234. A wide selection of fashionable clothes for men and women. There is also a snack bar.
Yves St. Laurent Rive Gauche 113 & 73 New Bond Street, W1; 493-1800. St. Laurent's ready-to-wear.
Zandra Rhodes 14A Grafton Street, W1; 499-3596. One of Britain's most successful and popular designers, renowned for her feminine chiffons.

BUSES

See TRANSPORTATION.

CHEESE SHOPS

The English love their cheese, and cheese-loving is easy to do here. In London you can sample not only all the British cheeses, but those from the continent and beyond as well. Some of the best places:
Dairy Center Covent Garden Market (Unit 4), WC2; 836-1662. Sample 1-ounce nibbles of unusual British cheeses for sale.

Harrods Knightsbridge, SW1; 730-1234. (See also DE-PARTMENT STORES.) In its unforgettable and grandly ornate Food Hall, as the grocery department is called, Harrods has more than 400 different kinds of cheese, including all the English ones.

Justin de Blank 42 Elizabeth Street, W1; 730-0605. A wonderful, high-class food store with an excellent selection of cheeses, including their own cheddar.

Paxton and Whitfield 93 Jermyn Street, SW1; 930-9892. Old-fashioned and quaint, Paxton's has been famous for years for its cheese (and its ham).

Selfridges Oxford Street, W1; 629-1234. (See also DE-PARTMENT STORES.) The cheese department is superior to the rest of the food hall in Selfridges, just as the food hall itself is superior to the rest of the store.

CHEMISTS

See DRUGSTORES.

CHILDREN'S LONDON

London has so many adult pleasures and attractions that you might think children would be a problem here. Not so. The city abounds in things that children love, too, and exploring London with a child is a special joy. Here are some ideas.

Babysitting Services

Babysitters Unlimited 313 Brompton Road, SW3; 584-1046. Carefully selected staff, with good references.

Brompton Bureau 10 Beauchamp Place, SW3; 584-6242. For 24-hour babysitting and mothers' helpers.

Childminders 67 Marylebone High Street, W1; 935-9763/935-2049. Reliable babysitting agency, willing to go to hotels as well as private houses.

Children

Gentle Ghost 27 Royal Crescent Mews, W11; 603-2871. A workers' cooperative without agency fees, offering a wide range of services including babysitting.
Universal Aunts 36 Walpole Street, SW3; 730-9834. Also reliable and willing to send sitters to hotels.
Visitors Welcome 17 Radley Mews, W8; 937-9755. Will take your children shopping or to the zoo. Interpreters if necessary.

Children's Clothing

Bananas 128A Northcote Road, SW11; 228-2384. A wide range of Scandinavian, French, American and English clothes for up to 8-year-olds. Also toys and books.
C and A 501–519 Oxford Street, W1; 629-7272. With branches all over town. A good, reliable place to buy a wide range of inexpensive children's clothing.
Children's Bazaar 162 Sloane Street, SW1; 730-8901. A good selection of second-hand clothing.
Colts 5 Hampstead High Street, NW3; 435-7387. Boys' casual clothes, well-made and reliable.
Marks and Spencer 458 Oxford Street, W1; 486-6207; other branches in various parts of town. British mums have been coming here for years. It's huge, it's cheap, it's good value.
Mothercare 461 Oxford Street, W1; 629-6621; many branches. A department store for children, with prams, bottles, and baby linen ans well as a full range of clothing.
Pollyanna 811 Fulham Road, SW6; 731-0673. Beautiful and unusual clothes for boys and girls up to 12.
Rowes 170 New Bond Street, W1; 409-1770. The opposite of Marks and Spencer, Rowes has outfitted generations of the very upper classes.
Small Wonder 296 King's Road, SW3; 352-9608. Clothes imported from the continent for children under 12.
Zero Four Plus 53 South Molton Street, W1; 493-4920. Expensive imported clothes for 0–14 years.

Children's Entertainment

Archaeological Digs The Council for British Archaeology, 112 Kennington Road, SE11; 582-0494. Publishes a monthly calendar of excavations in Britain where older children might find jobs as helpers.

Brass Rubbing St. James's Church Hall, Piccadilly (open 10–6), All Hallows Church beside the Tower of London (10:30–6), Westminster Abbey (9–5:30). An enjoyable way to get a bit of history to take home with you. Rates vary from 1 to 3 pounds.

Bus Rides There are many organized bus tours (see TOURS). But any child is thrilled by simply getting onto one of the 6,000 famous red double-deckers that ply the streets. Sit up top, as far forward as you can, and enjoy the show of London passing by.

Canal Trips Jason's Trip and Argonaut Gallery, across from 60 Bloomfield Road, W9; 286-3428. Has 1½-hour return trips, with commentary, through Regents Park and the Hampstead Road locks. Departures 11, 2, and 4:30. Also, Jenny Wren Cruises, 250 Camden High Street, NW1; 485-6210. 1½-hour cruises. As many as 4 trips a day at the height of the summer. Advisable to phone ahead for details, and to reserve a place.

Television Studios Write well ahead, enclosing a stamped, self-addressed envelope, and describing the sort of program you want to see. (Many are considered too sophisticated for children under 10; television in Britain is racier than it is in the United States.) For BBC, write to the Ticket Unit, Broadcasting House, W1. For ITV, write to Thames Television, 306 Euston Road, NW1, or London Weekend Television, Kent House, South Bank TV Centre, SE1.

Thames River Tours Phone 730-4812, the tourist board's special boat number, for schedules. Delightful when the weather is good, and a unique way to see London and learn its history. At the height of the summer season, there are regular boat services from Westminster Down River every 20 minutes or less. It takes 20 minutes to get to the Tower of London, and 50 minutes to get to Greenwich. Boats go up river from Westminster at least every half hour. The trip to Putney takes 30 minutes, to Kew 90 minutes. Longer trips to Richmond (2 hours, 30 minutes) and to Hampton Court (3 hours, 45 minutes) are of course less frequent. Many of the boats have useful commentaries, many have bars.

Children

Theater for Children

Dolphin Theater Company Shaw Theater, 100 Euston Road, NW1; 388-0031. Professional productions of Shakespeare as well as new playwrights.

Greenwich Young People's Theater Burrage Road, Plumstead, SE18; 854-1316. Imaginative shows in a converted church.

Little Angel Marionette Theater 14 Dagmar Passage, off Cross Street, N1; 226-1781. A delightful puppet theater, with both modern and traditional shows. The only permanent puppet theater in London.

Mermaid Theater Molecule Club Puddle Dock, EC4; 236-9521. Combining science and art, it aims to explain the physical principles of sound, energy, and light with artistic song and dance routines.

Round House Chalk Farm Road, NW1; 267-2564. Once a turntable for steam locomotives, this old theater has good productions. Saturday afternoons for the 5–12 set. Also programs at other times.

Unicorn Theater Club Arts Theater, Great Newport Street, WC2; 836-2574. Good plays for children aged 4–12. Interesting workshop.

Young Vic 66 The Cut, Waterloo, SE1; 928-6363. An offspring of the National Theater Company, with lively performances of Shakespeare and other classics. Also special children's plays.

Children's Museums

See also MUSEUMS.

Bethnal Green Museum Cambridge Heath Road, E2; 980-2415. Excellent collection of toys and doll houses. Open 10–6, Sundays 2:30–6.

Cutty Sark and Gipsy Moth Greenwich Pier, London SE10 (Greenwich); 853-3589. Two more old ships to climb around on. The *Cutty Sark*, built in 1869, was once the fastest clipper on the tea run from China; the *Gipsy Moth IV* is the 18-ton ketch in which Sir Francis Chichester sailed around the world in 274 days in 1966–1967. Open Mondays–Saturdays 11–6, on Sundays from 2:30. (Closes at 5 in the winter).

Geffrye Museum Kingsland Road, Shoreditch, E2; 739-8368. Housed in the former almshouses of the Ironmongers' Company, the Geffrye has historic furniture and woodwork from 1600 to modern times. The open-hearth kitchen is fascinating. Open daily 10–5, Sundays 2–5, closed Mondays.

H.M.S. Belfast Call 407-6434 for information. A real Navy gunship, the Belfast is not a floating museum. It is moored on the south bank of the Thames, roughly across from the Tower of London (there is a ferry service), and it offers a fascinating glimpse into life aboard a fighting cruiser, with filmed documentaries. Open daily from 11–4.

Imperial War Museum Lambeth Road, SE1; 735-8922. Awesome collection of implements of the 2 World Wars, from all over the British Empire. Open weekdays 10–5:50, Sundays from 2–5:50. Admission free.

London Dungeon 28–34 Tooley Street, SE1; 403-0606. An exhibition of the horrors of life in the Middle Ages in Britain. Sets depicting trials by ordeal, the murder of Becket, the Plague, the burnings of martyrs, and tortures galore. Kids love it, and don't mind that it is educational in the bargain. Open 7 days a week from 10–5:45 (from 10–4:30 in the winter).

London Planetarium Marylebone Road, NW1 (next door to Madame Tussaud's); 486-1121. Dazzling night sky; explains the sun, the moon, and the stars. Open 11–5:30. Also Laserium and Laserock concerts with laser light shows. Thursday–Sunday. (Phone for times.)

London Transport Museum across from the old Flower Market, Covent Garden, WC2; 379-6344. Every style of old bus and subway train is here, along with posters, models, working exhibits, and audiovisual displays as well. Open 10–6.

Madame Tussaud's Marylebone Road, NW1; 935-6861. Everybody loves it, from the walks through history to the surprise discovery that that tourist standing next to you is, in fact, wax. All the leading figures from every field are here, including many Americans. The chamber of horrors is particularly effective. Open from 10–6 (to 5:30 in the winter). Very long lines at the height of the season in the middle of the day, so try to get there early. And if you don't, well, go ahead and stand in line anyway; it's worth it.

National Army Museum Royal Hospital Road, SW3;

Children

730-0717. The proud history of the British Army from Tudor times until the First World War. Open 10–5:30; Sundays 2–5:30.

National Postal Museum King Edward Street, EC1; 432-3851. Marvelous display of British, Commonwealth, and foreign postal stamps from around the world, including artists' designs. Also special exhibitions about philately and postal history. Open Monday–Thursday, 10–4; Friday 10–4:30.

Pollock's Toy Museum 1 Scala Street, W1; 636-3452. Dolls, teddy bears, doll houses, all in a wonderful world for small children. Also toy theaters with colorful scenery. Mondays–Saturdays, 10–5. Closed Sundays.

Tower of London See ROYAL LONDON.

Playgrounds and Zoos

See also PARKS.

Adventure Playgrounds These unconventional parks consist of pieces of wood, construction materials, old cars, hunks of canvas, and other unusual contraptions, which children love to climb about on. To find the one nearest you, telephone 377-0314.

Battersea Park Children's Zoo Battersea Park, SW11; 228-2798. Children can walk right up and pat the goats, sheep, and deer—all very tame, but fun. Also exotic birds. Admission free. Open 12–late evening.

Crystal Palace Park SE19; 778–7148. Named after the 1851 Great Exhibition Building. It burned down in 1936, but the park is still a great attraction. On the boating lake, there are nearly 2 dozen life-size models of dinosaurs and other prehistoric animals. There is also a National Youth and Sports Center with an Olympic swimming pool and stadium. Open 8–dusk.

London Zoo Regent's Park, NW1. One of the world's great zoos, this one has something for everybody, including quite adequate eating and drinking facilities. To check on feeding times, telephone 722-3333. Children love the Zoo Farm, where they are allowed to pet cows, pigs, and goats and see how a farm works, including a milking demonstration. Opens daily 9 o'clock, closes about dusk.

Parliament Hill Southeast corner of Hampstead Heath (nowhere near Parliament, so don't be misled by the name). At 319 feet, it affords magnificent views of London. On windy days, especially Saturdays and Sundays, you will find dozens of people flying wonderfully colored exotic kites.

Round Pond Kensington Gardens; 937-4848. Right in front of Kensington Palace. Popular place for sailing model boats, with a playground for small children nearby. (In September, this area, like many other leafy parts of London, is crawling with small boys shaking "conkers"—a shiny kind of chestnut—out of the trees.)

CHOCOLATE AND CANDY

Bendicks 195 Sloane Street, SW1; 235-4749. One of the world's great chocolate producers, sinfully delicious.

Charbonnel et Walker 28 Old Bond Street, W1; 629-4396. Handmade chocolates for more than 100 years.

Clares 3 Park Road, NW1; 262-1906. Hand-made chocolate mints, creams, caramels.

Fortnum & Mason Piccadilly, W1; 734-8040. Wonderful candy department in a store that also has many other fine foods. Worth visiting, like a museum, even if you are not hungry.

Prestat 40 South Molton Street, W1; 629-4838. Brandy cherries, mints, truffles, and other elegant little treats. Expensive, but what the hell.

CLOTHING

See BOUTIQUES (WOMEN), HABERDASHERIES (men), and CHILDREN'S LONDON.

Chocolate

COFFEE AND TEA

Algerian Coffee Stores 52 Old Compton Street, W1; 437-2480. Has coffee and tea from a number of places (though *not* Algeria). Many special blends and grinds.
H. R. Higgins 42 South Molton Street, W1; 499-5912. Has blended and unblended coffees from around the world. Also coffee-making machines.
L. Fern 27 Rathbone Place, W1; 636-2237. Fern's blends its own and does a brisk mail-order trade as well.
Whittard & Co. 111 Fulham Road, SW3; 589-4261. Several dozen different teas on sale here as well as coffees from around the world. Smells wonderful.

DANCE
See MUSIC, OPERA, & DANCE.

DAYCARE
See CHILDREN'S LONDON.

DEPARTMENT STORES

London has all that you might expect for any big city in the way of shopping, but there are also a few department stores so special that they deserve mention. Of them, Harrods (see below) is the most outstanding.

Covent Garden Market WC2. Not really a department store, but rather more like an urban shopping center, in Covent Garden just north of the Strand. Several dozen extremely attractive shops on 3 levels, in the old covered market where fruit and vegetables used to be sold. (Henry Higgins met Eliza Doolittle, who became his Fair Lady, on the steps of the church just across the street.) A good deal of care has gone into the planning of the market, which opened in 1980, and a very high standard was applied in selecting the shops to be let in. It is good for just browsing, but here are a few special favorites: *Strangeways*, a far-out furnishings store that has such merchandise as lamps that look like fireplugs; *That's Entertainment*, a record store specializing in the scores of Broadway shows and movies (at last count, it had 6 *South Pacific*s and 3 *Oklahoma*s); *Pollock's Toy Museum*, for dolls, toys, and children's books; and *Parallax*, for startling glass mirrorware and neon interior decoration. There are several good restaurants in the area (see RESTAURANTS), so you can make a day of it.

Debenhams 344–8 Oxford Street, W1; 580-3000. Good selection of reasonably priced up-to-the-minute fashions, hosiery, cosmetics, kitchen goods and lingerie. The food hall in the basement is fairly comprehensive. Men's clothing too.

D. H. Evans 318 Oxford Street, W1; 629-8800. Ideal selection of clothes for the outsize and shorter woman, with an excellent lingerie department. Other generalized departments as well. Wools.

Dickins & Jones Regent Street, W1; 734-7070. Fashionable store, offering Continental and American women's clothes. Also men's clothes, household department, knitting wools. An excellent corsetry department.

Fenwicks 63 New Bond Street, W1; 629-9161. Women's, men's and children's wear. Good lingerie department. Terrace restaurant, hair and beauty salon, cosmetics and toiletries. There is a gift and cook shop in the basement, and they offer a very strong selection of accessories.

Fortnum & Mason 181 Piccadilly, W1; 734-8040. Best known for its sumptuous grocery department on the ground floor. Fortnum's also sells a wide range of luxury goods upstairs. A wonderful store to visit, even if you don't buy anything.

Department Stores

General Trading Company 144 Sloane Street, SW1; 730-0411. One of the finest stores in Britain, because of the high quality of its merchandise. Sells a wide range of furniture and furnishings, which you will find in London's best houses.

Harrods Knightsbridge, SW1; 730-1234. Surely one of the most wonderful department stores in the world. It claims to have everything, a claim that would be hard to disprove. (In fact, its registered cable address is EVERYTHING LONDON.) London's specialty shops are some of the finest in the world, true, but people who live here know that they are likely to find whatever they are looking for at Harrods.

Harvey Nichols Knightsbridge, SW1; 235-5000. Home furnishings, housewares, and smart clothes from top British, American and Continental designers.

John Lewis Oxford Street, W1; 629-7171. The largest selection of materials in Europe, for dresses and furnishings. An all-round department store, also offering an excellent range of china, glass and furniture.

Liberty & Co. Regent Street, W1; 734-1234. Their printed fabrics are famous. Oriental carpets, modern furniture and kitchen goods. They have a large glass and china department. Worth a visit for its fine architecture.

Marks & Spencer 173 & 458 Oxford Street, W1; 734-4904. With several dozen locations all over town. Beloved of the budget-conscious, this chain, known familiarly as "Marks and Sparks," has low-cost fashions for the whole family.

Peter Jones Sloane Square, SW1; 730-3434. A member of the John Lewis clan, this trendy store offers a large furnishings department, modern and antique furniture, china, glass and an excellent linen department. There is also a hairdressing salon.

Selfridges 400 Oxford Street at Orchard Street, W1; 629-1234. A general, all-purpose department store. No great distinction, but it has a wide range and a particularly good grocery department.

Simpsons 203 Piccadilly, W1; 734-2002. Eight floors offering smart luggage, knitwear, and sportswear.

DISCOS

See NIGHTLIFE, GAY SCENE.

DRUGSTORES

There are very few all-night chemists (British for "drugstores") left in London. In an emergency, call the police (999) and explain the problem. Here are a few, with hours:

Bliss Chemist 50–56 Willesden Lane, NW6; 624-8000. Open 24 hours, all week.

V. J. Hall 85 Shaftesbury Avenue, W1 (near Piccadilly Circus); 437-3174. Open till 11 every night. Sunday 12–10 P.M.

Warman-Freed 45 Golders Green Road, NW11; 455-4351. Open till midnight, 7 days a week.

W. W. Brunton 240 Earl's Court Road, SW5; 373-5078. Open till 10:30 every evening except Sunday. Open till 10 on Sunday.

EXCURSIONS OUT OF LONDON

Bath The only hot springs site in Britain, these were supposedly discovered by Bladud, father of Shakespeare's King Lear, in about 500 B.C. Bath is well known for its beautiful architecture, and has won countless awards for its magnificent horticultural and floral displays. Its beautiful landscape and setting on the River Avon combine to make Bath a town of tremendous natural beauty. It is also a cultural center with many varied events and theatrical productions being produced all year round. Additionally, the Bath Festival has become renowned as one of the most important music festivals throughout the United Kingdom. There is also a wonderful shopping center, where narrow streets and paved passages seem to enhance the shops with an even greater historical feel.

Brighton 50 miles. An easy, 90-minute train trip from Victoria Station brings you to this very interesting Atlantic City-type resort on England's south coast. Obviously, it is more pleasant when the weather is nice; there is an abundance of hotels and restaurants in every price range. The beach is not much by American standards, but it is fun to walk along the seafront, and to look at Brighton's fine Regency squares and terraces. Don't miss the Royal Pavilion, a fanciful palace built for George IV when he was still Prince Regent, with domes and pinnacles in oriental style. Brighton has good antique and curio shops.

Hampton Court 15 miles by train, half an hour from Waterloo Station. (Or go by boat up the Thames; see CHILDREN'S LONDON.) A splendid Tudor palace built beginning in 1514 by Cardinal Wolsey. Henry VIII took it over from the Cardinal and added a great hall and chapel, and lived much of his life in the palace. It was added to by later monarchs, and is now a kind of architectural museum, reflecting architectural standards over the centuries. It also now possesses a number of royal art collections, and has a pleasant garden for picnicking.

Oxford 63 miles by train, a 1-hour trip from Paddington Station. Seat of one of the world's great universities, through which you can wander rather freely, getting a feel for its antiquity and its excellence. Also the home of Blackwell's, one of the best bookstores in Britain, scattered around a warren of little shops in the center of town. Blenheim Palace, home of the Duke of Marlborough and birthplace of Winston Churchill, is just 8 miles away, outside Woodstock.

Stratford-on-Avon 121 miles, 2½ hours by train. (Or a bit less time if you go by car, a pleasant drive through beautiful rolling country.) Once there, you find the town a kind of living museum to William Shakespeare, who was born there in 1564. It is also a very agreeable little place, but the main attraction, of course, is the Royal Shakespeare Theater, which now

Excursions

has a season that lasts most of the year. Many good hotels and restaurants.

Windsor 20 miles. Half an hour or so by bus, 1 hour by train. Windsor Castle has been the home of English kings since at least the times of Henry I, and possibly earlier. A huge, gray stone fortress, the castle is visible from miles away, dominating the little town, which is also appealing, with its ancient, narrow streets. Visit the splendid State Apartments, which are still used by the Royal Family, and the Queen's Doll House, a perfect, fully working model palace that was given to Queen Mary in 1924. Eton—the home of Eton College, the famous private school—is just a short walk from the center of Oxford (on the other side of the bridge that crosses the Thames). The stunningly beautiful 15th-century Eton chapel is open to the public in the afternoon.

FABRIC SHOPS

The Fabric Shop 6 Cale Street, SW2; 584-8495. Excellent range of designers works, many originals.

Habitat 206 King's Road, SW3; 351-1211. Many branches over town, offering a wide selection of out-of-the-ordinary fabrics.

Heals 196 Tottenham Court Road, W1; 636-1666. An interesting store in itself, but their fabric department offers a superb choice of modern fabrics in every type of design and weave imaginable.

Liberty & Co. Regent Street, W1; 734-1234. Liberty began selling fine Japanese silks 100 years ago, and they are still at it, upholding an international reputation for excellence and style. They are also noted for their cotton lawns. Most Liberty fabrics are now British, though, and their designs are still first-rate.

Arthur Sanderson & Sons 52 Berners Street, W1; 636-7800. Well known for their coordinated designs and colorful selections.

Fabric

GARDENS
See PARKS.

GAY SCENE

Although homosexual relationships between consulting adults are no longer illegal in Britain, the gay scene in London tends to be restrained and private, by the standards of American cities or Northern Europe. The best source of information is *Gay News*, a literate and informative biweekly newspaper, which is sold on many newstands in Central London. It contains a calendar of events and a guide to bars, clubs, and restaurants. Private clubs are often open to foreign tourists, on presentation of a passport. It seems that many more pubs have discotheques, but these are not specified under the Pubs section. However, more details can be obtained by ringing Gay Switchboard. Here follows a listing by postal area of Pubs, Discos, Clubs and Disco/Clubs.

Pubs

W1
Ace of Clubs 52 Piccadilly; 499-4296 (women only).
City of Quebec Old Quebec Street; 629-6159.

W6
Royal Oak 62 Glenthorne Road; 748-2781.

W11
Champion 1 Wellington Terrace; 229-5056.

WC2
Salisbury 90 St. Martin's Lane; 836-5863.

N1

King Edward VI 25 Bromfield Street, Islington; 359-1121.
The Bell 259 Pentonville Road; 837-5617 (women only).

NW1

Euston Tavern 73 Euston Road; 387-4566.
Laurel Tree 113 Bayham Street at Greenland Street; 485-1383.
New Black Cap 171 Camden High Street; 485-1742.
Sols Arms 65 Hampstead Road; 387-3721 (women's disco).
Traffic 126 York Way; 837-6012.

NW3

King William IV 77 High Street, Hampstead; 435-5747.

E2

Alternative 34 Red Church Street; 739-2808 (women only).

EC1

London Apprentice 333 Old Street; 739-5577.

SW1

Pig & Whistle Little Chester Mews; 235-3438 (Sunday lunch only).

SW3

Markham Arms King's Road; (No phone number as yet) (Saturday lunch only).
Queen's Head Tryon Street, off King's Road; 589-0262.

SW4

The Two Brewers 114 Clapham High Street; 622-3621.

Gay Scene

SW5

Chaps & Bromptons 294 Old Brompton Road; 373-6559. (Two separate bars).
Coleherne 261 Old Brompton Road; 373-5881.

SW8

Market Tavern The Market Tower, 1 Nine Elms Lane; 622-5655.

SW10

Boltons Old Brompton Road at Earl's Court Road; 373-9172.

SW11

Cricketers Battersea Park Road; 622-9060.

SE1

Crown 108 Blackfriars Road; 928-4269.

SE5

Union Tavern 146 Camberwell New Road; 735-3605.

SE11

Royal Vauxhall Tavern 372 Kennington Lane; 382-0833.

SE16

Ship & Whale 2 Gulliver Street; 237-3305.

Discos

WC1

Drill Hall 16 Chenie Street; 637-8270 (women only Mondays).

WC2

Bangs 157 Charing Cross Road; 734-6963 (Monday and Thursday).

N1

Kanes 348 Caledonian Road; 607-9701 (for women).

N8

Bolts at Lazers 6–9 Salisbury Promenade, Green Lanes; 802-5959.

N17

Beryl's at Valentino 344 High Road, Tottenham; 808-0691. (For women, Saturdays).

NW1

Femme The Cock, 2 Diana Place, Triton Square; 387-3865 (Women only, Saturdays).

E3

Benjy's 562A Mile End Road; 980-1991.

E11

Selina's 575 High Road, Leytonstone; 539-0766.

E15

Pigeons Hotel 120 Romford Road, Stratford Road; 534-1955 (Saturdays only).

SE15

Kings 132 Peckham Rye; 390-1556 (for women).
Pat's Parlour Canterbury Arms, 871 Old Kent Road; 639-3827.

Gay Scene

Clubs

W1

Appollo 31 Wardour Street; 437-7301.
Burlington Health 23 Old Bond Street; 409-2989.
Oscar's 4 Greek Street; 437-9446.

W8

Sombrero 142 Kensington High Street; 937-2096.

WC2

Cellar 182 Hungerford Lane, Craven Street; 839-4252 (leathers).
Festival 2 Brydges Place, St. Martin's Lane; 836-1436.

SW3

Gateways 239 King's Road (enter from Bramerton Street); 352-0118 (women only).

SW5

Copa's 84 180 Earl's Court Road; 373-3407.

SW7

Copocabana 3 Cromwell Road; 584-7258 (Sundays only).

Disco/Clubs

W1

Napoleons & Bonaparte Restaurant 2 Lancashire Court, 123 New Bond Street; 493-3075 (48-hour wait for membership).
Spats 37 Oxford Street; 437-7945.

Gay Scene

W11

Gate (above Rymans) 68 Notting Hill Gate; 229-0161 (membership essential).

WC2

Heaven The Arches, Villiers Street, Charing Cross; 839-3862.
Hippodrome Coventry Street, Charing Cross; 437-4311 (Mondays only).
Stallions 5–6 Falconberg Court, off Charing Cross; 437-0047 (Tea dance on Sundays 5–8 P.M.).

Organizations

Campaign for Homosexual Equality 274 Upper Street, N1; 359-3973.
Gay Authors Workshop 79 Mitcham Road, E6; 471-7040.
Gemma Group for Disabled Lesbians BM Box 5700, WC1.
National Council for Civil Liberties 21 Tabard Street, SE1; 403-3888.
National Union of Students Gay Liberation Campaign 461 Holloway Road, N7; 272-8900.

Counseling and Advice

Albany Trust 24 Chester Square, SW1; 730-5871.
Gay Christian Movement Enquiries on 283-5165 (evenings only).
Gay Legal Advice 821-7672. Nightly from 7–10.
Gay Switchboard 837-7324. 24-hour service.
Icebreakers 274-9590. A group for isolated or lonely gay people. 7:30 P.M.–10:30 P.M.
Lesbian Line 837-8602, or write BM Box 1514, WC1N 3XX. Monday–Friday, 2 P.M.–10 P.M., Tuesday–Thursday 7 P.M.–10 P.M.
London Friend 274 Upper Street, Islington, N1; 359-7371. 7:30 P.M.–10 P.M.
Parents Enquiry 16 Honley Road, Catford, SE6; 698-1815. Counseling for parents of young gays.
Sigma 837-7324. Support for straight people in mixed relationships.

Gay Scene

Gay Travel Agencies
Man Around Ltd. Suite D, 9 Thorpe Close, Portobello Green, W10; 969-1122.
Uranian Travel 313 Old Brompton Road, SW3; 584-6558.

GOURMET FOODS
See BAKERIES AND PASTRY SHOPS, CHEESE SHOPS.

GYMS
See SPORTS AND SPORTING EVENTS.

HABERDASHERIES

Shopping for clothes in London is no longer the bargain that it once was for American men. But it is still lots of fun, because of an assortment that ranges from the $1,000 to $2,000 handmade ("bespoke") suits of Savile Row to the junk of Oxford Street. What follows is a selection, from many different kinds of shops:

Aquascutum 100 Regent Street, W1; 734-6090. A huge selection of high-quality clothing of all kinds.
Austin Reed 103 Regent Street, W1; 734-6789. Good-quality suits, haberdashery. Five shopping floors.
Burberrys Ltd. 18 Haymarket, SW1; 930-3343, and 165 Regent Street, W1; 734-4060. World-famous for their raincoats, of course, but Burberrys has a wide selection of other clothes as well.

Burtons 114 Regent Street, W1; 734-1951. Good suits and shirts at cheaper prices.
Carnaby Street Soho, W1. Made famous in the 1960s, the boutiques of Carnaby Street are now pretty trashy, but you can still find some way-out fashions.
Jaeger 204 Regent Street, W1; 734-8211. High-quality clothing for both men and women.
Les 2 Zebras 38 Tavistock Street, WC2; 836-2855. Very chic, very high-style continental suits and accessories.
Lilywhites Piccadilly Circus, W1; 930-3181. Wonderful selection of sporting clothing. And if they don't have what you are looking for, they'll get it for you.
Scotch House 2 Brompton Road, SW1; 581-2151, and 187 Oxford Street, W1; 734-8802, and 84 Regent Street, W1; 734-0203, and 191 Regent Street, W1; 734-4816. High-quality woolens and tweeds for both men and women. Americans will find shetland sweaters at what seem like bargain prices (one of the few shopping bargains left in all of London).
Turnbull & Asser 71 Jermyn Street, SW1; 930-0502. Very, very expensive manufacturer of high-quality shirts, ties, robes, and such for the Mayfair man-about-town. In a very toney neighborhood that is worth browsing through, even for the unfashionable.

HOSPITALS AND HEALTH EMERGENCIES

The basic advice is to call 999 for any emergency service and ask the operator for the service you require—i.e., police, fire, ambulance. You will then be connected to their central number. You do not need a coin to make this call from a public phone. The following hospitals have 24-hour casualty, or emergency, service.
Middlesex Hospital Mortimer Street, W1; 636-8333.
New Charing Cross Hospital Fulham Palace Road, W6; 748-2040.

Royal Free Hospital Pond Street, NW3; 794-0500.
St. Bartholomew's Hospital West Smithfield, EC1; 600-9000.
St. Stephen's Hospital, 369 Fulham Road, SW10; 352-8161.
University College Hospital Gower Street, W1; 387-9300.
Westminster Hospital Dean Ryle Street, Horseferry Road, SW1; 828-9811.

HOTELS

It is unwise to arrive in London without a hotel reservation. But if you do, you can find out what is available by going to the London Tourist Board's Accommodation Service. It is in Victoria Station, SW1, near platform 15. You can pay as much as £100 for a night, or as little as £10. In the following list, which is selective, hotel prices are indicated by letter ratings. The price for a room with bath for 2 persons (including tax and breakfast) is:

A more than £85
B £65–£85
C £45–£65
D £35–£45
E £25–£35
F under £25

Not surprisingly, you get what you pay for. Hotels in the E and F categories, though clean and comfortable, are distinctly not deluxe, and few of them offer the range of services that you can expect in the higher-priced hotels. Many of the cheapest places listed here are in the bed and breakfast tradition, in which the only meal offered is breakfast and the only public room is the breakfast room.

Alexander Hotel 9 Sumner Place, SW7; 581-1591 (C). A very good bargain hotel made from 3 terraced houses.

PICCADILLY CIRCUS

Alison House Hotel 82 Ebury Street, SW1; 730-9529 (E). A small, friendly place well situated near Victoria Station.

Apollo Hotel 18 Lexham Gardens, W8; 373-3236 (F). A pleasant, unpretentious hotel made from a converted Victorian terraced house.

Athenaeum Hotel 116 Piccadilly, W1; 499-3464 (A). A very modern luxury hotel overlooking Green Park. It has a very good, extremely elegant restaurant.

Atlas Hotel 24 Lexham Gardens, W8; 373-7873 (F). A small and friendly bargain hotel just off Cromwell Road.

Bardon Lodge 15 Stratheden Road, Blackheath, SE3; 853-4051 (E). A cheerful bed-and-breakfast place near Greenwich Park.

Barkston Hotel Barkston Gardens, SW5; 373-7851 (D). A friendly old Victorian hotel, a bit on the tatty side, but comfortable.

Basil Street Hotel 8 Basil Street, SW3; 581-3311 (B). Elegant and grand, with a mahogany staircase and antiques in the public rooms.

Berkeley Hotel Wilton Place, SW1; 235-6000 (A). One of London's grandest hotels, discreet and rich. Very good, and very elegant restaurant.

Blake's Hotel 33 Roland Gardens, SW7; 370-6701 (A). Very stylish and fashionable hotel made out of a row of old Victorian houses. Bedrooms are beautifully furnished, though many are small, and the place seems overpriced. The lovely restaurant, with fresh tulips on the tables, is top-notch at dinner time, and attracts a very trendy crowd.

Bloomsbury Center Hotel Coram Street, Russell Square, WC1; 837-1200 (C). Popular with businessmen and tour groups. No character particularly, but it gets the job done.

Bonnington Hotel 92 Southampton Row, WC1; 242-2828 (C). Friendly and very clean, with brightly painted bedrooms. Something of a bargain.

Bristol Hotel Berkeley Street, W1; 493-8282 (A). A very efficient modern hotel with smart service and decor.

Britannia Hotel Grosvenor Square, W1; 629-9400 (B). A grand and stylish hotel in the swankiest part of Mayfair.

Brown's Hotel Dover Street, W1; 493-6020 (A). An elegant, terraced hotel with an unhurried, 19th-century mood. Its good restaurant is well-suited to a leisurely meal.

Cadogan Hotel Sloane Street, SW1; 235-7141 (B). Red brick, turreted building with big, comfortable rooms.

Capital Hotel 22 Basil Street, SW3; 589-5171 (A). Smart and modern hotel on a quiet street in Knightsbridge. Good restaurant.

Carlton Tower Hotel Cadogan Place, SW1; 235-5411 (A). High-style and modern. Rooms on upper floors have sweeping views of some of the best neighborhoods in London.

Cavendish Hotel Jermyn Street, SW1; 930-2111 (B). Busy, bustling hotel on one of London's most fashionable shopping streets.

Central Park Hotel 49 Queensborough Terrace, W2; 229-2424 (D). Just across from Kensington Gardens, and near the shopping on Kensington High Street.

Century Hotel 18 Craven Hill Gardens, W2; 262-6644 (E). Attractively furnished rooms at bargain prices.

Charing Cross Hotel Strand, WC2; 839-7282 (C). A grand old railway hotel above Charing Cross station. Heavy glass chandeliers and deep easy chairs, it recalls Victorian days.

Chesham House Hotel 64 Ebury Street, SW1; 730-8513 (E). A simple and modest hotel, well run at lowest prices.

Chesterfield Hotel 35 Charles Street, W1; 491-2622 (B). Converted town house built in 1742 by the fourth Earl of Chesterfield, it still has an air of quiet opulence about it.

Churchill Hotel Portman Square, W1; 486-5800 (A). A sleek, modern hotel with the highest of standards, though not much character. Convenient to Oxford Street shopping.

Claridge's Brook Street, W1; 629-8860 (A). One of the very best in town, favored by presidents and kings. Art deco design in the public rooms and bedrooms. Lovely restaurant.

Clive's Hotel Primrose Hill Road, NW3; 586-2233 (C). Functional and efficient, with good conference facilities. Popular with business people.

Coburg Hotel 129 Bayswater Road, W2; 229-3654 (C). A grand old place on the north side of Hyde Park, with domes and Edwardian paneling.

Colin House Hotel 104 Ebury Street, SW1; 730-8513 (E). A typical, and quite effective, conversion from Victorian terraced houses, for the traveler on a tight budget.

Colonnade Hotel 2 Warrington Crescent, W9; 289-2167 (D). A large and comfortable hotel, popular with tourists.

Columbia Hotel 95 Lancaster Gate, W2; 402-0021 (E). A dignified hotel overlooking Hyde Park. Large comfortable rooms.

Concord Hotel 157 Cromwell Road, SW5; 370-4151 (E). Two Victorian terraced houses converted into a friendly and comfortable, low-priced hotel.

Connaught Hotel Carlos Place, W1; 499-7070 (A). Quite simply, one of the best hotels in the world, possessing one of the finest restaurants. Grand, old-world, understated, it is favored by people accustomed to the best.

Cranley Gardens Hotel 8 Cranley Gardens, SW7; 373-3232 (E). Another of the attractively converted Victorian terraced houses. Pleasant and friendly.

Craven Gardens Hotel 16 Leinster Terrace, W2; 262-3167 (E). Modern, efficient rooms, behind a striking Georgian façade. Very comfortable.

Culford House 9 Culford Gardens, SW3; 581-3255 (E). Small, unpretentious hotel off the King's Road.

Cumberland Hotel Marble Arch, W1; 262-1234 (B). A big, busy hotel at the end of Oxford Street. Well-equipped bedrooms.

Curzon Hotel Stanhope Lane, Park Lane, W1; 493-7222 (C). A medium-size, modern hotel on a quiet street in Mayfair.

Diplomat Hotel 2 Chesham Street, SW1; 235-1544 (D). Atmosphere of faded elegance, with marble floors and circular staircase.

Dorchester Park Lane, W1; 629-8888 (A). One of the best. Elegant and stylish, with outstanding restaurant.

Drury Lane Hotel 10 Drury Lane, High Holborn, WC2; 836-6666 (B). A modern, concrete and glass structure in the heart of the theater district.

Duke's Hotel 35 St. James's Place, SW1; 491-4840 (A). Discreet and smart, Duke's is tucked away on a quiet street just south of Piccadilly with the air of a good men's club.

Durrant's Hotel 26 George Street, W1; 935-8131 (C). A comfortable and roomy old place which is able to be something of a bargain because of its relatively unfashionable (though not particularly inconvenient) location north of Oxford Street.

Edbury Court Hotel 26 Ebury Street, SW1; 730-8147 (C). A charming little hotel near Victoria Station.

Eden House Hotel 111 Old Church Street, SW3; 352-3403 (D). Converted Edwardian house on a quiet street in Chelsea. Especially suited for families.

Eden Park Hotel Inverness Terrace, W2; 229-1453 (D). Slightly tatty, but good for the bargain seeker.

Eden Plaza Hotel 68 Queen's Gate, SW7; 370-6111 (D). At the corner of Cromwell Road, convenient to South Kensington's museums.

Elizabeth Hotel 37 Eccleston Square, SW1; 828-6812 (D). On a quiet square in a good part of town, the Elizabeth offers modest accommodation, at bargain prices.

Elizabetta Hotel 162 Cromwell Road, SW5; 370-4282 (D). Modern, glass and concrete. Functional and efficient.

Embassy House Hotel 31 Queen's Gate, SW7; 584-7222 (C). Nineteenth-century townhouse completely modernized inside. Bright, pleasant rooms.

Europa Hotel Grosvenor Square, W1; 493-1232 (A). Luxurious and elegant, with well-designed rooms. Very good and very elegant.

Executive Hotel 57 Pont Street, SW1; 581-2424 (D). Only a discreet brass plaque on the outside tells you that you are there. Once inside, you find a bright, friendly place with bedrooms of varying sizes.

Forum Hotel 97 Cromwell Road, SW7; 370-5757 (C). A huge-24-story, American-style hotel, very modern and efficient. Very good panoramic views of Kensington and beyond from the upper floors.

Frognal Lodge Hotel 14 Frognal Gardens, NW3; 435-8238 (D). An attractive converted private house in a quiet spot in beautiful Hampstead.

Garden Court Hotel 30 Kensington Gardens Square, W2; 229-2553 (F). Simply decorated, pleasant rooms in an unpretentious but friendly little place.

George Hotel 58 Cartwright Gardens, WC1; 387-1528 (E). Friendly, family-run hotel in an interesting neighborhood near Bloomsbury.

Gloucester Hotel Harrington Gardens, SW7; 373-6030 (A). Modern and well-run hotel. Popular with Wimbledon players during the tournament.

Goring Hotel 15 Beeston Place, Grosvenor Gardens, SW1; 834-8211 (B). A comfortable, old-world hotel

Hotels

which gives very good value for money.

Grand Eastern Hotel Liverpool Street, EC2; 283-4363 (D). Another of the wonderfully old-fashioned railway hotels. This one is convenient to the City, London's financial district.

Great Northern Hotel King's Cross, N1; 837-5454 (C). Victorian style and lots of space, both in the public rooms and in the bedrooms.

Great Western Royal House Praed Street, W2; 723-8064 (C). Like the other railway hotels, it recalls the 19th century, and an unhurried, pre-aviation era in which the train was king.

Grosvenor Court Hotel 144 Praed Street, W2; 262-3464 (D). A functional and agreeable hotel behind a Victorian façade near Paddington Station.

Grosvenor Hotel 101 Buckingham Palace Road, SW1; 834-9494 (C). Not to be confused with the much more elegant Grosvenor House, below. This one is a grand old 19th-century building next to Victoria Station. Though a bit down-at-heel, it is comfortable.

Grosvenor House Park Lane, W1; 499-6363 (A). Busy and stylish, with comfortable, luxurious rooms.

Harewood Hotel Harewood Row, NW1; 262-2707 (D). A modern, brick hotel near Marylebone Station. Good value, though not a very good location for the tourist.

Hendon Hall Hotel Ashley Lane, Hendon, NW4; 203-3341 (D). A red-brick Georgian building that was once the home of David Garrick, the actor.

Henry VIII Hotel 19 Leinster Gardens, W2; 262-0117 (D). Well-modernized Victorian building with good, comfortable rooms. Good value.

Hilton International Kensington Holland Park Avenue, W11; 603-3355 (B). A modern, American-style hotel with a good Japanese restaurant in the lobby.

Hilton International London 22 Park Lane, W1; 493-8000 (A). A classic example of the Hilton style, in a tall, modern building with good views over Hyde Park, Mayfair, and Belgravia.

Hogarth Hotel 35 Hogarth Road, SW5; 370-6831 (E). A pleasant, modern hotel, with functional rooms.

Holiday Inn There are 3 of them: Sloane Street, SW1; 235-4377 (A). 134 George Street, W1, 723-1277 (A); and 128 King Henry's Road, NW3, 722-7711 (B). All are modern and efficiently run, in the style of Holiday Inns the world over.

Hospitality Inn (Bayswater) 104 Bayswater Road, W2; 262-4461 (C). A tall, concrete hotel in the American style. Not very imaginative, but comfortable, with good views of Hyde Park.

Hotel 128 128 Holland Road, W14; 602-3395 (F). Delightful and attractive little place. Very well run, and tastefully decorated. A bargain.

Howard Hotel Temple Place, Strand, WC2; 836-3555 (A). A modern, concrete hotel with some spectacular views of the Thames. Convenient to law offices.

Hyde Park Hotel Knightsbridge, SW1; 235-2000 (A). One of the best of the old-style, marble-and-polish, with an enviable position overlooking Hyde Park, and a quietly elegant restaurant.

Imperial Hotel Russell Square, WC1; 837-3655 (D). A modern hotel with well-equipped rooms. Interesting, bookish neighborhood.

Inn on the Park Hamilton Place, Park Lane, W1; 499-0888 (A). Efficient and well-run, modern hotel.

Inter-Continental Hotel 1 Hamilton Place, W1; 409-3131 (A). Popular with business people (especially on expense accounts).

Ivanhoe Hotel Bloomsbury Street, WC1; 636-5601 (C). A stunning old Victorian building with very simple rooms. Most do not have bathrooms, but if you don't mind that, it is a good bargain.

Jenkin's Hotel 45 Cartwright Gardens, WC1; 387-2067 (F). A small, modest hotel on a pleasant terrace near Russell Square. Friendly service, family-run.

John Howard Hotel 4 Queen's Gate, SW7; 581-3011 (A). A small and smart hotel in one of South Kensington's lovely old terraces.

Kennedy Hotel 43 Cardington Street, NW1; 387-4400 (C). A modern hotel near Euston Station.

Kensington Close Hotel Wright's Lane, W8; 937-8170 (C). A cheerful and enormous hotel just off Kensington High Street. Good value.

Kensington Palace Hotel De Vere Gardens, W8; 937-8121 (B). A comfortable place overlooking Kensington Gardens.

Kingsley Hotel Bloomsbury Way, WC1; 242-5881 (D). A popular hotel near the British Museum. Simply decorated, but good value.

Knightsbridge Green Hotel 159 Knightsbridge, SW1; 584-6274 (C). Comfortable accommodation, mostly in suites, in this former apartment house. Very good location for smart shopping.

L'Hotel 28 Basil Street, SW3; 589-6286 (C). Clean and pleasant 4-story building in a very stylish part of town.

Ladbroke Kensington Court Hotel 33 Nevern Place, SW5; 370-5151 (D). No great character, but a good deal of comfort, in large-well-equipped rooms.

Lancaster Court Hotel 202 Sussex Gardens, W2; 402-8438 (E). A simple, terraced hotel near Paddington Station. Not fancy, but good value.

Leicester Court Hotel 41 Queen's Gate Gardens, SW7; 584-0512 (D). Five-story, terraced house with big, airy rooms and a bright, friendly atmosphere. Few rooms have their own bathrooms.

Leinster Towers Hotel Leinster Gardens, W2; 262-4591 (E). Once the home of the Duke of Leinster, this striking building is now a comfortable hotel with a bit of luxury still in the air.

Lexham Hotel 32 Lexham Gardens, W8; 373-6471 (E). Four adjoining houses converted into a pleasant hotel with an attractive garden.

Lily Hotel 23 Lillie Road, SW6; 381-1881 (E). Modern, well-equipped hotel convenient to Earl's Court Exhibition Center.

London Belgravia Hotel 20 Chesham Place, SW1; 235-6040 (A). A comfortable, modern hotel in the heart of Belgravia.

London Embassy Hotel 150 Bayswater Road, W2; 229-1212 (C). Modern and smart, with all amenities. The hotel has a terrace facing Kensington Gardens.

London International Hotel 147 Cromwell Road, SW5; 370-4200 (C). A glass and marble high-rise, American-style hotel. You get good views of Kensington from the top.

London Metropole Edgware Road, W2; 402-4141 (C). A modern hotel not far from Marble Arch. Popular with tour groups. It is stylishly decorated, with comfortable bedrooms.

London Tara Hotel Scarsdale Place, Wright's Lane, W8; 937-7211 (C). Modern, bright, and huge. Near Kensington High Street. Popular with tour groups.

Londoner Hotel Welbeck Street, W1; 935-4442 (C). Convenient to Oxford Street shopping and many of the standard sights of the city, this pleasant hotel is popular with tourists.

Lowndes Hotel Lowndes Street, SW1; 235-6020 (A). Fully deluxe, modern hotel on a quiet street in most chic Belgravia. Discreetly well run.

Manor Court Hotel 35 Courtfield Gardens, SW5; 373-8585 (E). Terraced hotel with comfortable, if nonelegant accommodation for the budget-conscious.

Mayfair Hotel Berkeley Street, W1; 629-7777 (A). Very stylish and elegant, this hotel in the center of Mayfair offers every comfort and luxury.

Merryfield House. 42 York Street, W1; 935-8326 (E). Tiny, comfortable little terraced hotel, well run and cosy.

Milford House 31 York Street, W1; 935-1935 (E). A Georgian town house with only 6 rooms. They are well maintained and bright, though only one of them has a private bath.

Montague Hotel Montague Street, WC1; 637-1001 (E). A pleasant and comfortable hotel near the British Museum.

Montcalm Hotel Great Cumberland Place, W1; 402-4288 (A). Very well-appointed and handsome hotel behind an elegant, terraced Georgian façade near Marble Arch. Bedrooms include some split-level suites. Very elegant, with a luxurious and well-run restaurant.

Mount Royal Hotel Bryanston Street, W1; 629-8040 (C). A large, modern hotel with bright, cheerful rooms. All have walk-in dressing rooms and tiled bathrooms.

New Berners Hotel Berners Street, W1; 636-1629 (B). Large, comfortable hotel with charming galleried entrance and recently renovated rooms.

New Mandeville Hotel Mandeville Place, W1; 935-5599 (B). Recently renovated, this hotel has small, but comfortable rooms and a friendly, welcoming atmosphere.

Number Sixteen 16 Sumner Place, SW7; 589-5232 (C). Number Sixteen has a loyal and regular clientele, who keep on coming back because they appreciate the atmosphere of a well-appointed private home. Like visiting someone rather grand in his home.

Oliver Hotel 198 Cromwell Road, SW5; 370-6881 (E). A pleasant, medium-sized hotel in a well-modernized old building.

Park Lane Hotel Piccadilly, W1; 499-6321 (A). One of the grand old hotels, the Park Lane has retained its sense of luxury, though it is a bit tatty at the edges. Pleasant and comfortable mood, with piano player in the lobby bar.

Park Plaza Hotel Lancaster Gate, W2; 262-5022 (D). Comfortable hotel in the area north of the park, which is popular with tour groups and others on a budget. Striking Edwardian façade.

Parkwood Hotel 4 Stanhope Place W2; 402-2241 (D). A modernized Victorian terraced house just by Marble Arch and Hyde Park. Cheerfully decorated and well-furnished rooms make this place a bargain.

Pastoria Hotel St. Martin's Street, WC2; 930-8641 (C). Well situated near the National Gallery. Cosy rooms with built-in units.

Pembridge Court Hotel 34 Pembridge Gardens, W2; 229-9977. (D). A converted Victorian house with bright, well-renovated bedrooms. Comfortable.

Philbeach Hotel 30 Philbeach Gardens, SW5; 373-1244 (E). A pleasant place, in a peaceful crescent near the Earl's Court Exhibition Center.

Piccadilly Hotel Piccadilly, W1; 734-8000 (B). A striking Victorian Building with pillars and rich panels that recall the last century, but modernized, comfortable bedrooms.

Portman Inter-Continental Hotel 22 Portman Square, W1; 486-5844 (A). A sleek, modern brick hotel on a pleasant square just north of Oxford Street. Well-equipped for business people.

Portobello Hotel 22 Stanley Gardens, W11; 727-2777 (C). A particularly successful conversion of a Victorian terrace, very attractively furnished and well run.

Post House Hotel (Hampstead) 215 Haverstock Hill, NW3; 794-8121 (C). A 6-story, modern building, well furnished, and brightly decorated, with a comfortable mood.

President Hotel Russell Square, WC1; 278-7871 (D). Modern and efficient, the President is popular with students and group tours. It is well situated in one of the most interesting neighborhoods in town. Good value.

Prince Hotel 6 Sumner Place, SW7; 589-6488 (E). An elegant, terraced house. Very comfortable, but no private baths.

Queensbury Court Hotel 9 Queensbury Place, SW7; 589-3693 (E). Three terraced houses converted into a comfortable hotel. Well run with friendly service. Near the museums of South Kensington.

Regent Crest Hotel Carburton Street, W1; 388-2300 (C). A modern, efficient hotel.

Rembrandt Hotel 11 Thurloe Place, SW7; 589-8100 (C). Gracious, 100-year-old hotel near the Victoria and Albert Museum.

Ritz Hotel Piccadilly, W1; 493-8181 (A). One of the half dozen best hotels in London. Superb in every detail. The dining room is one of the prettiest in town, sumptuous and elegant.

Royal Angus Hotel 39 Coventry Street, W1; 930-4033 (C). Overlooking Leicester Square, the Royal Angus is convenient to theaters and West End shopping.

Royal Garden Hotel Kensington High Street, W8; 937-8000 (A). Luxurious and modern hotel, with balconies overlooking Kensington Gardens. The rooftop restaurant has panoramic views and sophisticated, well-prepared food.

Royal Horseguards Hotel Whitehall Court, SW1; 839-3400 (C). A converted, Victorian apartment house, convenient to Parliament and the government offices in Whitehall.

Royal Lancaster Hotel Lancaster Terrace, W2; 262-6737 (A). A modern, American-style high-rise hotel with good views of Kensington Gardens.

Royal National Hotel Bedford Way, WC1; 637-2488 (E). Clean, modern, and functional. A good bargain.

Royal Park Hotel 5 Westbourne Terrace, W2; 402-6187 (F). Converted from a Victorian terrace near Paddington Station.

Royal Scot Hotel 100 King's Cross Road, WC1; 278-2434 (C). Simple bedrooms with built-in units. Two floors reserved for nonsmokers.

Royal Trafalgar Hotel Whitcomb Street, WC2; 930-4477 (C). Comfortable and modern, with an ideal location for the sightseer.

Royal Westminster Hotel Buckingham Palace Road, SW1; 834-1302 (C). Modern hotel near Victoria Station. Besides its regular rooms, it has 18 luxury suites each stylishly fitted to a particular theme.

Ruskin Hotel 23 Montague Street, WC1; 636-7388 (F). In a pleasant row of terraced houses near the British Museum. A bargain.

Russell Hotel Russell Square, WC1; 837-6470 (C). A splendid old place that has retained its 19th-century charm. Overlooking the square, in one of London's most interesting neighborhoods.

St. Ermin's Hotel Caxton Street, SW1; 222-7888 (D).

Well-situated, turn-of-the-century hotel, with opulent public rooms, rather ordinary bedrooms.

St. George's Hotel Langham Place, Oxford Circus; W1, 580-0111 (C). A modern and efficient businessperson's hotel with panoramic views of London.

Savoy Hotel Strand, WC2; 836-4343 (B). One of London's very grandest hotels. The lobby is opulently marble, the views of the river are peaceful, and the service is impeccable. The stylish Grill Room and the River Room overlooking the Thames are both top-quality restaurants.

Selfridge Thistle Hotel Orchard Street, W1; 408-2080 (B). A modern and efficient hotel near the busy Selfridge's department store, but well removed from its bustle and noise.

Sheraton Park Tower 101 Knightsbridge, SW1; 235-8050 (A). A luxurious, modern, 17-story hotel in the heart of stylish Knightsbridge. Very elegant restaurant called Le Trianon.

Stafford Hotel St. James's Place, SW1; 493-0111 (A). Very quiet and stylish hotel tucked away on a back street south of Piccadilly. First-rate service.

Stanhope Court Hotel 46 Stanhope Gardens, SW7; 370-2161 (D). A large, well-maintained hotel near the Victoria and Albert. Comfortable, quiet rooms.

Strand Palace Hotel Strand, WC2; 836-8080 (C). A huge, gray stone building popular with businesspeople and tourists because of its location halfway down the Strand.

Stratford Court Hotel 350 Oxford Street, W1; 629-7474 (D). Comfortable rooms with fitted units. In the heart of the West End.

Surtees Hotel 94 Warwick Way, SW1; 834-7163 (F). Cheerful and modest little hotel near Victoria Station.

Swiss Cottage Hotel 4 Adamson Road, NW3; 722-2281 (D). Part of a grand old Victorian terrace, opulently furnished with fine oil paintings and antique furniture.

Tavistock Hotel Tavistock Square, WC1; 636-8383 (E). A large, red-brick hotel on one of London's pleasant squares.

Tower Hotel St. Katharine's Way, E1; 481-2575 (B). Very modern, efficient and well-equipped with good views of the river. The location, near the Tower of London, is difficult for most tourists, but convenient for business people visiting the city.

Tudor Court Hotel 60 Cromwell Road, SW7; 584-8273 (D). Cheerful bargain spot in the middle of South Kensington.

Waldorf Hotel Aldwych, WC2; 836-2400 (B). Elegant and luxurious old Edwardian hotel, with a charm that survived recent renovation.

Washington Hotel Curzon Street, W1; 499-7030 (C). Nicely maintained, though not as fashionable as the neighborhood that it is in.

West Centre Hotel 47 Lillie Road, SW6; 385-1255 (D). A tall, modern hotel convenient to the Earl's Court Exhibition Centre.

Westbury Hotel New Bond Street, W1; 629-7755 (A). A sleek, modern hotel with high standards.

Westmoreland Hotel at Lords Lodge Road, St. John's Wood, NW8; 722-7722 (C). Close to the Lords cricket ground. Modern and efficient.

White House Hotel Albany Street, NW1; 387-1200 (B). Converted apartment house, the White House offers friendly service and comfortable accommodation near Regent's Park. Its pleasant restaurant has good French cooking.

White's Hotel 90 Lancaster Gate, W2; 262-2711 (C). A handsome Victorian hotel facing Kensington Gardens. Attractively decorated rooms.

Wilbraham Hotel 1 Wilbraham Place, SW1; 730-8296 (C). Old-fashioned, friendly, and charming, with a very regular and loyal clientele.

Willett House Hotel 32 Sloane Gardens, SW1; 730-0634 (E). A friendly, owner-managed, bargain spot just off Sloane Square.

INFORMATION

See also NEWSPAPERS AND MAGAZINES.

American Embassy 24 Grosvenor Square, W1; 499-9000. The place to go if you have no money, have lost your passport, or need legal advice.

British Rail Travel Centre 12 Regent Street, SW1 (no phone enquiries). Booking center for travel all over Britain, and rail-sea journeys to the continent. Other, smaller offices are at 14 Kingsgate Parade, Victoria Street, SW1; 407 Oxford Street, W1; 170B Strand, WC2, and 87 King William Street, EC4.

British Tourist Authority 64 St. James's Street, SW1; 499-9325. A first-rate service for tourists, with mountains of literature and brochures, some free, some for sale. Nine languages spoken, all questions cheerfully answered. Open from 9–6 weekdays and 9–2:30 on Saturdays in the summer and from 9:15–5:30 weekdays and 9:15–12:30 on Saturdays in the winter.

Citizens Advice Bureaux (for free advice on any practical problem), 32 Queen Street, EC4; 74 Marchmont Street, WC1; Westminster Council House, Marylebone Road, NW1; 99 Tachbrook Street, SW1; 33 Charing Cross Road, WC2.

City of London Information Center For information specifically about the square mile known as "The City," which includes St. Paul's Cathedral and the financial district, St. Paul's Churchyard, EC4; 606-3030. Free literature, and very useful monthly Diary of Events, which is a guide to what's going on in the oldest part of London.

Daily Telegraph Information Service (telephone enquiries only, on any subject), 353-4242. From 9:30–5:30 weekdays only.

Emergency help For police, fire, ambulance, dial 999

Guildhall Library Aldermanbury EC2; 606-3030. For information about any aspect of London's history, 9:30–5. Monday–Saturday.

London Tourist Board Information Center Victoria Station, SW1; 730-0791. Travel and tourist information about London: times, places, dates. Very good, efficient, and helpful. Open 9–8:30 weekdays and 9–5 on Sunday.

London Transport Travel Enquiry Offices Stop by for a "How to Get There" booklet in any of 6 languages, or telephone 222-1234, 24 hours a day. Offices are in the following underground stations: St. James's Park, Charing Cross, Euston Station, Heathrow, King's Cross, Oxford Circus, Piccadilly Circus, Victoria Station, and Waterloo. All are open from 8:30 A.M.—9:30 P.M., 7 days a week. For information about the Green

Line coaches, which go out into the countryside, telephone 834-6563, or visit the office at Eccleston Bridge, Victoria, SW1, 8–5.

Telephone Services

Dial 142 for directory assistance in Greater London, 192 for the rest of the country, including both parts of Ireland. Dial 100 to reach the operator. Internal telegrams have now been replaced by telemessage and take a day longer to arrive! Their number is 190. International telegrams, dial 193. You can now dial directly to the United States and many other countries, as well as within Britain. Check the little green booklet "Telephone Dialing Codes," which is usually with the 4-part London telephone directories. There are also a good many recorded messages that you can dial in London:
Bedtime stories, 246-8000
Children's London, 246-8007
Business news and the Financial Times index of stock prices, 246-8026
Horse racing, 168
Sportsline, 246-8020
Teledata (for what's on, shops, services, garages, businesses, etc.), 24-hour service, 200-0200.
Discline, 246-8008.
Motoring information, 246-8021
Recipe for the day, 246-8071
Tourist information, 246-8041.
Weather forecast, 246-8091
Time, 123

JEWELRY SHOPS

For all the perennial talk about the poverty of Britain, it has some of the world's finest jewelry, and somebody must be buying the stuff. Whether you are in the market for a million-dollar necklace, or just browsing, thanks, here are the best places to look.

Andrew Grima 80 Jermyn Street, W1; 839-7561. Every piece in this fascinating shop is unique, and there is an imaginative use of gemstones.

Asprey & Co. 165 New Bond Street, W1; 493-6767. One of the finest and most famous shops in London, not only for jewelry, but for high-class household merchandise as well. Top drawer.

Booty 9 New Bond Street, W1; 629-6796. Also 14 Holborn, EC1; 242-1891. Beautiful jewelry, much of it by young artists.

Cartier 175 New Bond Street, W1; 493-6962. With branches at 20 Albermarle Street, W1, and in the lobby of the Intercontinental. The London outlet of the internationally famous jeweler is as sumptuous as its other branches.

Collingwood 12 Kingsgate Parade, SW1; 828-2968. Just a stone's throw from Buckingham Palace, which is appropriate since this shop has long been a supplier to royalty.

Cutler Street Silver Market Off Houndsditch, E1. A street market primarily for dealers, specializing in jewelry, most of it silver. Also some coins and medals. Sunday mornings, starting at dawn.

Editions Graphiques 3 Clifford Street, W1; 734-3944. Art nouveau and art deco jewelry in a serious, untrendy setting.

Garrard 112 Regent Street, W1; 734-7020. Calls itself "the crown jewellers," and not without cause. A recent Garrard commission was to make both the wedding ring and the engagement ring that Prince Charles gave his bride in 1981.

LANDMARKS

See SIGHTS WORTH SEEING.

LEATHER GOODS

Alfred Dunhill 30 Duke Street, SW1; 499-9566. World-famous name for tobacco, Dunhill's also has a stunning range of high-quality bags and wallets.
Gucci 27 Old Bond Street, W1; 629-2716. A very fashionable shop with the famous Italian leather goods.
Henry's 201 Regent Street, W1; 437-6579 and 185 Brompton Road, SW3; 589-2011. Handbags, wallets, carry-alls in imaginative design. High quality.
Loewe 25 Old Bond Street, W1; 493-3914. Wonderfully rich Spanish leather and suede. Coats made to order.
Swaine, Adeney, Brigg & Sons 185 Piccadilly, W1; 734-4277. A grand, old-fashioned place that calls itself a whip and umbrella manufacturer, this shop also has very high-quality luggage.

LIMOUSINES

(Chauffeur-driven)

Arthur Monk 677 Finchley Road, NW2; 794-8111. Also has minibuses.
Hanover Car Hire 8 Alfred Place, WC1; 580-0505.
Patrick Barthropp 1 Dorset Mews, Wilton Street, SW1; 245-9171.

MARKETS

Outdoor or open-air markets are a fascinating part of the city's texture, even if you don't want to buy. Here's a selection.

Arches Villiers Street, WC2. Not really an outdoor market, but rather a line of stalls and shops selling militaria, fire brigade and police items, coins, stamps, medallions, and bric-a-brac.

Bermondsey and New Caledonian Market Between Tower Bridge and Bermondsey Street, SE1. Antiques and junk, for dealers and collectors and also browsers. Fascinating assortment. Open 7 A.M.–1 P.M., Fridays only.

Berwick Street Soho, W1. Beautiful vegetables. Monday to Saturday 9 A.M.–6 P.M.

Brick Lane Brick Lane, E1. Mostly household junk, but you can find some interesting merchandise if you rummage around. Sundays from 5:30–9.

Camden Passage Islington High Street, N1. Flea market on Wednesday mornings, where they sell antiques and junk and antique junk. Monday to Saturday, 9 A.M.–6 P.M.

Chelsea Antiques 253 Kings Road, SW3. Large market, mostly offering generalized stock, but with some specialists. Monday to Saturday, from 8 A.M.

Club Row Sclater Street, E1. Puppies, hamsters, guinea pigs, kittens, fish for sale. Animal protection groups are campaigning to get this market closed, on the grounds that it is cruel to the animals. The RSPCA, however, are seeing to it that the animals are well looked after. Open Sunday mornings.

Cutler Street Silver Market Houndsditch, E1. Mostly for dealers. Silver jewelry, coins, medals. Sunday mornings, beginning at dawn.

Greenwich Antiques Market Greenwich High Road, SE10. Every Saturday, opposite St. Alfege's Church. 8 A.M.–4 P.M.

Leadenhall Street Market Gracechurch Street, EC3. Retail fruit and vegetables, poultry, fish, meat. Many small shops with different opening times but generally Monday to Friday, 9 A.M.–5 P.M.

WESTMINSTER ABBEY

Leather Lane Holborn, EC1. A great lunchtime market (weekdays) close to Hatton Garden, the diamond center (comparable to West 47th Street in New York City). A little bit of everything, some of which, undoubtedly, "fell off the back of a lorry," as thieves here sometimes say. Monday to Friday, 11 A.M.–3 P.M.

London Silver Vaults Chancery Lane, WC2. An underground cave packed with modern and antique silverware. Monday to Friday, 9 A.M.–5:30 P.M., Saturdays 9 A.M.–12:30 P.M.

New Caledonian Tower Bridge Road, Bermondsey, SE1. Mostly for dealers—antiques, other furniture, bric-a-brac, silver. Fridays, beginning at dawn.

New Covent Garden (wholesale) Nine Elms, SW8. London's leading fruit, vegetable, and flower market. Still fun and lively, but a good deal of the charm was lost in the move from the old Covent Garden Market (which is now a very attractive complex of retail shops; see DEPARTMENT STORES). Open Monday to Sunday from 4 A.M. Flower market on Saturdays, but only in the summer.

Petticoat Lane Middlesex Street, E1. An enormous market selling all manner of household merchandise, some of it presumably stolen, most of it junk. Sundays from 9 A.M.–2 P.M.

Portobello Road Notting Hill Gate, W11. Furniture, furnishings, funny clothes, bric-a-brac, antiques. A lot of junk, some of it quite bizarre, and rather little of quality. But it's still fun. Monday through Saturday, beginning at 9.

Smithfield (wholesale) Charterhouse Street, EC1. A beautiful old building, built in 1867 by Sir Horace Jones, housing one of the world's largest meat markets. If huge piles of raw, bloody meat offend you, give this one a miss. Weekday mornings from 5 o'clock.

Spitalfields (wholesale) Commercial Street, E1. Five-acre covered fruit and vegetable market. Monday through Saturday from 4:30 in the morning.

Whitechapel Market Whitechapel, E1. Famous East End market, with a huge array of stalls. Monday to Saturday, 8 A.M.–5 P.M.

MOVIE THEATERS

There are dozens of motion picture theaters in the center of London, and many more in the residential outskirts, showing every kind of film. American movies are sometimes cut a bit, because censorship for general release tends to be a bit stricter in Britain. Films are rated as follows: U—General exhibition. 15—For anyone aged 15 and over. 18—Restricted to people 18 or over. PG—For general exhibition but parents are advised that the film may include material unsuitable for young children. You can find out what is playing at the general cinemas by checking the daily newspapers or *Time Out*. What follows is a listing of some of the specialized houses.

Academy 165 Oxford Street, W1. Three cinemas in 1 house, all specializing in sophisticated international fare. The films of Satyijat Ray, the noted Indian director, for example. They have 3 different phone numbers: 437-2981, 437-5129, and 437-8819.

Camden Plaza 211 Camden High Street, NW1; 485-2443. A broad choice of contemporary and often unusual films, some intellectual, some trendy.

Curzon Curzon Street, W1; 499-3737. Sumptuous surroundings showing carefully selected new films.

Electric Screen 191 Portobello Road, W11; 229-3694. Shows hundreds of old movies a year, including almost certainly some of your favorites.

Essential Cinema Club 76 Wardour Street, W1; 439-3657. Changes its program every day. Musicals and recent classics, such as *Casablanca*.

Everyman Cinema Holly Bush Vale, off Heath Street, NW3; 435-1525. Revivals of quality movies that you may have missed the first time.

Gate Cinema 87 Notting Hill Gate, W11; 727-5750. Interesting new films, classic and foreign, plus some old favorites, especially at late-night showings.

Gate 2 Cinema Bloomsbury Centre, Brunswick Square, WC1; 837-8402. The same sort of films as the other Gate (see above).

Institute of Contemporary Arts (ICA) Nash House, The Mall, SW1; 930-6393. Broad range of unusual films, some controversial.

Little Bit Ritzy Brixton Oval, Coldharbor Lane, SW2; 737-2121. Alternative, antiestablishment films and experimental.
London Film-makers Co-op 42 Gloucester Avenue, NW1; 586-4806. A film workshop too, and some of its films are made by members.
Minema (New Berkeley Hotel) 45 Knightsbridge, SW1; 235-4225. A very small cinema showing modern classics.
National Film Theater South Bank, SE1; 928-3232. Some of the best of the old film classics. The theater also has retrospective revivals of a particular director or a certain star. A very comfortable theater that is part of the South Bank complex.
Screen on the Green Islington Green, N1; 226-3520. New films not in general release, and old classics.
Screen on the Hill 230 Haverstock Hill, NW3; 435-3366. Unusual films that you won't see in general release.

MUSEUMS

London has a museum for just about every subject, some private, some public, some tiny, some vast. Excluding children's museums which are under CHILDREN'S LONDON; here is a sampling.

Art Museums

London is, of course, one of the world's major art centers, and you could spend your life here going to museums. Here is a list of the major ones. Admission is free, unless noted. (See also CHILDREN'S LONDON for museums especially for young people but which are delightful for grownups too.)
Banqueting House Whitehall, SW1. Superb example of Palladian architecture erected by Inigo Jones in

1625. Charles I was hanged here in 1649, but the chief attraction now is Rubens' magnificent allegorical paintings on the ceiling. Open Tuesday–Saturday, 10–5; Sundays 2–5. Admission charge.

Courtauld Institute Gallery Woburn Square, WC1; 580-1015. An outstanding collection of French impressionists, including Cezanne, van Gogh, and Gauguin, and modern paintings. Open daily 10–5, Sunday 2–5.

Foundling Hospital (Thomas Coram Foundation for Children). 40 Brunswick Square, WC1; 278-1911. Small gallery of 18th-century painters, including Hogarth, Gainsborough, and Kneller. Open 10–4, Monday–Friday only.

Geffrye Museum Kingsland Road, E2; 739-8368. Period rooms and furniture from the 17th century to the present day. Also 18th-century almshouses. Tuesday to Saturday 10–5, Sunday 2–5.

Hayward Gallery Belvedere Road (in the South Bank arts center), SE1; 928-3144. The Gallery has major exhibitions from all over the world. Consult the newspaper to see what's on. Open 10–8 Monday–Thursday, 10–6 Friday and Saturday, and 12–6 Sunday. Admission charge.

Heinz Gallery 21 Portman Square, W1; 580-5533. Regular exhibitions of architectural drawings. Open 11–5 Monday–Friday, 10–1 Saturdays, closed on Sundays.

Hogarth House Hogarth Lane, Great West Road, W4; 994-6757. Home of the 18th-century artist, William Hogarth, now a museum of his engravings. Open weekdays (except Tuesday) 11–6, Sundays 2–6. (Winter hours: 11–4 weekdays, except Tuesday, 2–4 Sundays. They are closed for three weeks over the Christmas period.)

Institute of Contemporary Arts Nash House, The Mall, SW1; 839-5344. Various temporary exhibitions on different aspects of contemporary arts. Also cinema (see MOVIES). Open 12–8 Tuesday–Sunday.

Iveagh Bequest, Kenwood Kenwood House, Hampstead Lane, NW3; 348-1286. Splendid Adam house containing paints by Rembrandt, Reynolds, Gainsborough, Vermeer and Turner. Open 10–7 every day from April through September, 10–4 from October–March, and 10–4 from November–February.

Leighton House 12 Holland Park Road, W14; 602-3316. Oriental tiles from the middle ages, paintings by Burne-Jones, Watts and De Morgan pottery. Open 11–5 Monday–Saturday.

National Gallery Trafalgar Square, WC2; 839-3321. Italian, Dutch, Flemish, Spanish, German and French painting before 1900, as well as British painters from Hogarth to Turner. Said to contain at least one masterpiece by every major European painter of the last five centuries. Open weekdays 10–6, Sundays 2–6.

National Portrait Gallery 2 St. Martin's Place, Trafalgar Square, WC2 (adjacent to the National Gallery); 930-1552. Prints, drawings, busts of famous Britons over the centuries. The most recent major addition is Bryan Organ's portrait of Diana, Princess of Wales. Open Monday–Friday, 10–5, Saturday 10–6 and Sunday 2–6.

Percival David Foundation of Chinese Art 53 Gordon Square, WC1; 387-3909. Chinese ceramics from the Sung to Ch'ing dynasty. Reference library. Open Monday 2–5, Tuesday–Friday 10:30–5, Saturday 10:30–1 (but not in August). Closed on Sundays.

Photographers' Gallery 8 Great Newport Street, WC2; 836-7860. Stunning photographs by some of the best photographers. Open 11–5 Monday–Saturday.

Queen's Gallery Buckingham Palace Road, SW1 (adjoining Buckingham Palace on the south side); 930-4832. Rotating exhibition drawn from Queen Elizabeth's huge private art collection. Open weekdays (except Monday) 11–5, Sundays 2–5. Admission charge.

Royal Academy of Arts Burlington House, Piccadilly, W1; 734-9052. A huge temple of traditional art, with thrilling special exhibitions that boggle the mind. They hold yearly summer exhibitions in May, showing works of present-day artists.

Serpentine Gallery Kensington Gardens, W8; 402-6075. A little gallery inside the park (near the body of water known, because of its shape, as the Serpentine), it has changing exhibitions of modern sculpture, painting and drawing. 10–7 April–September, Monday–Sunday. Winter 10–dusk.

South London Art Gallery Millbank, SW1 (on river bank, a 10-minute walk south from Parliament); 821-1313. Primarily devoted to British artists, especially Turner, Blake and the Pre-Raphaelites. Open daily 10–6, Sunday 2–6.

Victoria and Albert Museum Cromwell Road, SW7; 589-6371. A huge and wonderful museum with a vast collection covering almost every aspect of the decorative arts. Plus special exhibitions. Important collections of paintings, sculpture, graphics, typography, as well as armor, weapons, carpets, ceramics, clocks, costumes, and on and on and on. Don't miss it. Monday–Thursday and Saturday 10–5:50. Sunday 2:30–5:50.

Wallace Collection Hertford House, Manchester Square, W1; 935-0687. A gem of a museum in what used to be a grand and elegant private house. Exceptionally fine works of Dutch, Flemish, French, Italian, and British painters, as well as sculpture, furniture and china. The famous 'Laughing Cavalier' by Frans Hals is here. The museum is of manageable size and does not overwhelm. Open daily 10–5, Sunday 2–5.

Whitechapel Art Gallery 80 Whitechapel High Street, E1; 377-0107. Frequently changing exhibitions, usually of modern art. Open 11–6 Sunday–Friday, 11–7:50 Thursday. Free on Monday after 2.

Other Museums

Artillery Museum The Rotunda, Woolwich Common, SE18; 856-5533. Notable collection of guns and muskets. Open 10–12:45 and 2–5 Monday to Saturday, 2–5 Sunday.

Battle of Britain Museum Grahame Park Way, NW9; 205-2266. A memorial to the people in the great air battle of 1940. Open 10–6 weekdays, 2–6 Sundays.

Bear Garden Museum 1 Bear Garden, Bankside, SE1; 928-6342. A permanent exhibition on Elizabethan theater, in a converted 18th-century warehouse. April–December 10:30–6, Friday–Sunday. By appointment only for Wednesdays and Thursdays. February–March, again by appointment only. Closed in January.

British Museum Great Russell Street, WC1; 636-1555. Perhaps the single most important institution of its kind in the world. You could spend your life in it. (Some scholars do.) It has everything—prints, drawings, coins, medals, Egyptian and Assyrian antiquities, Greek, Roman, British, Mediaeval, Oriental antiquities, and a library. Open weekdays 10–5, Sundays 2:30–6.

British Piano and Musical Museum 368 High Street, Brentford, Middlesex; 560-8108. Two hundred musical instruments, including pianos, organs, musical boxes, dulcimers, and violins. And they all really work. Also old phonographs. Open 2–5, Saturdays and Sundays from April–October.

Broadcasting Gallery 70 Brompton Road, SW3; 584-7011. A museum of radio and television broadcasting. See how it all works, and how it all evolved. Open by appointment and guided tour only.

Commonwealth Institute 230 Kensington High Street, W8; 602-4535. Displays reflecting all aspects of life in the countries that used to be part of the British Empire. Also a cinema and art exhibitions. Open 10–5:30 Monday–Saturday, 2:30–6 on Sundays.

Dickens House 48 Doughty Street, WC1; 405-2127. Occupied by Dickens from 1837–1838, this house has been made into a wonderful museum and shrine recalling his life and his works. You can see first editions, letters, portraits, and furniture he used. Admission charge. Monday–Saturday 10–5 (last visitor admitted at 4:30). Closed Sundays.

Fenton House Hampstead Grove, NW3; 435-3471. The Benton Fletcher collection of early keyboard instruments, and the Binning collection of porcelain and furniture. Open Monday, Wednesday, Friday, and Saturdays 11–5, Sundays 2–5 during April–November. Closed from December–March.

Geological Museum Exhibition Road, SW7; 589-3444. Gemstones, other minerals and exhibitions relating to basic earth science and geology. Open daily 10–6, Sundays 2:30–6.

Goldsmiths' Hall Foster Lane, EC2; 606-8971. An elaborate collection of antique plate, and one of the largest collections of modern silver and jewelry in the country. By appointment only.

Gordon Medical Museum St. Thomas Street, SE1; 407-7600. Specimens and models relating to human disease. Admission by application to the Curator.

Gunnersbury Park Museum Gunnersbury Park, Popes Lane, W3; 992-1612. Local museum on the history of Chiswick, Brentford and Ealing, in west London. Good archaeological and topographical displays. Open 2–5 Monday–Friday.

Dr. Johnson's House 17 Gough Square, EC4. Home of the great lexicographer from 1748 to 1759, this neat little house is now a museum devoted to his life and his work. Tucked away on a quiet square behind the bustle of Fleet Street. Open 11–5:30 daily, closed Sundays. Admission charge.

Keats House Keats Grove, NW3. The home of John Keats during the most creative years of his short life. On a quiet residential street in Hampstead. Beautiful garden (in which he wrote his ode, "To a Nightingale," one fine spring morning in 1819) and exhibits relating to his work. Open daily from 10–6, Sundays from 2–5.

London Dungeon Tooley Street, SE1; 403-0606. Realistic exhibitions on horrible things, such as the Great Plague. For young boys and others who relish horror. Open daily 10–5:45 (10–4:30 during the winter). Admission charge.

MCC Memorial Gallery Lords Cricket Ground, NW8; 289-1611. A museum on the history of cricket, fascinating to lovers of the sport. Open 10:30–5 Monday–Saturday. Other times by appointment.

Museum of London London Wall, EC2; 600-3699. A wonderfully complete museum on every aspect of London's long history. Fascinating for residents and tourists alike. Open 10–6 Tuesday–Saturday, 2–6 on Sundays.

Museum of Mankind 6 Burlington Gardens, W1 (behind the Royal Academy); 437-2224. Anthropology in an appealing and exciting setting. All kinds of tribal life from around the world are explained and displayed. Open weekdays from 10–5, Sundays from 2:30–6.

National Maritime Museum Romney Road, Greenwich, SE10; 858-4422. A truly superb and very complete museum of everything pertaining to the sea (about which, you will recall, the British have traditionally known quite a bit). Ship models, paintings, navigation instruments, charts, medals, naval uniforms, and some of the grand old vessels in which the Royal Family used to ride up and down the Thames. A wonderful museum. Open 10–6 Tuesday–Saturday, 2–5:30 Sundays. Closed Mondays. In the winter, open from 10–5 Tuesday–Saturday, and 2–5 Sundays.

Natural History Museum Cromwell Road, SW7; 589-6323. Wonderful collections of zoology, entomology, paleontology and botany. Huge dinosaur models and a particularly educational display on human biology and sexuality. You could spend all day there. Open 10–6 weekdays, 2:30–6 on Sundays.

Passmore Edwards Museum Romford Road, E15; 519-4296. Very good collections of Essex archaeology, local history from geological and biological point of view. Impressive collection of Bow porcelain. Open 10–6 Monday–Friday, 10–8 Thursdays, 10–1 and 2–5 Saturdays. Closed Sundays.

ALBERT HALL

Pharmaceutical Society's Museum 1 Lambeth High Street, SE1; 735-9141. Pharmaceutical instruments over the years, and ancient apparatus. By appointment only.

Public Record Office Museum Chancery Lane, WC2; 405-0741. Historical records and documents, including the Domesday Book and two versions of Magna Carta. Open Monday–Friday 9:30–5.

Royal Air Force Museum Aerodrome Road, Hendon, NW9; 205-2266. (15 minutes' walk from the Colindale Station on the Northern tube line.) A huge museum devoted to the R.A.F. in all its glory. Real airplanes trace the history and development of military aviation. Many exhibits explaining the intricacies of such things as jet fighters, and walk-in displays. Good for children. Open 10–6 Monday–Saturday, 2–6 Sundays.

Royal College of Music Prince Consort Road, SW7; 589-3643. Ancient musical instruments, including a 450-year-old harpsichord. Open (during term-time) 10:30–4:30. Mondays and Wednesdays by appointment only.

Royal College of Surgeons The Hunterian Museum, Lincolns Inn Fields, WC2; 405-3474. Displays on physiology, anatomy, and pathology. Open 10–5 Monday–Friday. Closed during August. In theory, it is just for doctors.

St. Bride's Crypt St. Bride's Church, Fleet Street, EC4; 353-1301. Interesting displays of artifacts found during the excavation of this part of town. Insights into what used to be Roman London. Open 9–5 every day.

St. Bride Printing Library St. Bride Institute, Bride Lane, EC4; 353-4660. Early printing equipment, machinery, and books. Open 9–5:30, Monday–Friday. By appointment only.

Science Museum Exhibition Road, SW7; 589-3456. A huge and wonderful temple to the sciences with comprehensive displays on physics, chemistry, mathematics, engineering, mining, and transportation. Originals of locomotives, aircraft, and cars. Open daily 10–6, Sundays 2:30–6.

Wellcome Historical Medical Museum 183 Euston Road, NW1; 387-4477. Medicine and surgery over the centuries. Open Monday–Friday, 10–5. Closed at weekends. Strictly for the medical profession.

Wellington Museum 149 Piccadilly (Hyde Park Corner), W1; 499-5676. The London home of the famous Duke of Wellington (His address was simply, "Number 1, London".) It contains decorations, trophies, paintings, and uniforms mostly related to him. Open Tuesday to Thursday and Saturday 10–6, Sundays 2:30–6.

Wimbledon Tennis Museum Church Road, SW19; 946-2244. Displays of everything related to tennis through the years—drawings, equipment, dresses, and uniforms—and a good library of books about tennis. Open 11–5 Tuesday–Saturday, 2–5 Sunday.

Music, Opera & Dance

You can see and hear some of the world's best in London, in an astonishing range from the traditional and classical to far-out punk rock. For band concerts in the parks, see PARKS. For information, also try the **Greater London Arts Association**, 25–31 Tavistock Place, WC1; 388-2211. They provide information on modern dance performances; also leads to where to find classes and workshops.

Here are the high spots for serious music.

Coliseum St. Martin's Lane, WC2; 836-3161. A huge theater, seating 2,400. The home of the English National Opera, which does opera in English, and is also used by visiting companies.

Covent Garden Royal Opera House Floral Street, WC2; 240-1066. The home of the Royal Ballet and the Royal Opera company. A theater of unforgettable grandeur. Both companies have an international reputation for the excellence of their productions. Many performances are sold out, so it is wise to plan ahead. Program information available by phone 24 hours.

Place 17 Duke's Road, WC1; 387-0161. An unusual and exciting modern dance company.

Purcell Room South Bank, SE1; 928-3191 for bookings and 928-3002 for information. Part of the South Bank arts complex. For chamber music and solo concerts.

Queen Elizabeth Hall South Bank, SE1; same phone numbers as the Purcell Room. Chamber music, choral concerts, poetry readings.

Royal Albert Hall Kensington Gore, SW7; 589-8212. Wonderful old Victorian domed hall built in 1871 and named after her late husband. All kinds of music here—pop, orchestral, *Messiah* at Christmastime, the popular "proms" concerts—as well as public meetings.

Royal College of Music Prince Consort Road, SW7; 589-3643. Chamber music and orchestral concerts.

Royal Festival Hall South Bank, SE1; 928-3191 for bookings, 928-3002 for information. The largest of the auditoriums in the complex.

Sadler's Wells Theatre Rosebery Avenue, EC1; 837-1672. Originally the home of the Royal Ballet, Sadler's Wells is now used by visiting ballet and opera companies.

St. John's Smith Square, SW1; 222-1061. A lovely 18th-century church now used for concerts and recitals.

Wigmore Hall 36 Wigmore Street, W1; 935-2141. Instrumental recitals, chamber music, vocalists.

Musical Instruments

Bill Lewington 144 Shaftesbury Avenue, WC2; 240-0584. A good selection of both new and secondhand instruments.

Boosey & Hawkes 295 Regent Street, W1; 580-2060. Manufactures brass and woodwind instruments, also violins.

Henry Keat 32 Clarence Mews, Clarence Road, E5; 985-5673. Secondhand brass instruments, repairs. Also bugles and coaching horns.

J. Broadwood & Sons 60 Buckingham Palace Road, SW1; 730-7419. A wide range of pianos.

Paxman 116 Long Acre, WC2; 240-3642. A very well-known manufacturer of horns. Also does repairs, and sells sheet music.

Salvi Harps 55 Endell Street, WC2; 836-0788. Manufactures and sells beautiful harps.

Newspapers and Magazines

Unlike American cities, London has a great wealth of daily newspapers. Visitors to the city can find out a good bit about it, and about what is going on here, by reading them, especially the serious, quality papers. Here is a short sketch.

The Times It is incomparable, still one of the world's greatest newspapers, even under the ownership of Rupert Murdoch. Unlike most others, it makes a serious effort to keep its news columns objective, the way American newspapers do. Its slip-out Preview section every Friday is a useful guide to the arts and entertainment.

The Financial Times (The salmon-colored one.) Primarily for the financial and business community, but it also has excellent coverage of the arts.

The Guardian No longer the *Manchester Guardian*, but still liberal, it cares about things that some others ignore, such as domestic poverty, race relations, the third world. Excellent arts coverage.

The Daily Telegraph Strictly Tory with an imperial view of the world (including Ireland).

Daily Mail Strictly Tory tabloid on the borderline between the quality dailies and the popular press ("the qualities" and "the pops," in Fleet Street slang). Nigel Dempster's daily gossip column is must reading for the smart set.

Daily Express Once distinguished, now no longer.

Daily Mirror, Daily Star, The Sun Virtually identical tabloids, with a steady diet of sex, sensationalism, trivia, and idle gossip about Charles and Diana. Not worth buying.

There is also quite an array of weekly magazines designed to provide consumer and entertainment news to Londoners. At this writing, they are having a bit of a circulation war, and it is unlikely that they will all survive it. But the present lineup looks like this.

City Limits New magazine recently launched by defectors from the staff of *Time Out*. More strident in its left-wing politics, with a lot of information about po-

litical protest marches and such.
Event Especially big on sound, with reviews of new popular music.
Illustrated London News Glossy and rich, this one is aimed at upper-middle-class Belgravia and Chelsea types.
Time Out Informative and authoritative. Especially thorough look at what's playing at the movies.
What's On in London Thorough and established. A bit less trendy, more middle-aged in its outlook than *Time Out*.
Where to Go A lot on nightlife, including quite a bit on so-called adult entertainment, massage parlors, escort services.

NIGHTLIFE

For most Britons, nightlife seldom consists of anything more exciting than a visit to the neighborhood pub. And a warm and wonderful experience that can be. (See PUBS.) But lately, London has acquired a somewhat swinging late-evening scene, centering on supper clubs, discotheques, and private clubs, which have proliferated in response to liquor laws that require the pubs to close at 11. Some of these private clubs are genuinely private. (For example, Annabel's in Berkeley Square, one of the most prestigious and attractive late-night spots in town, has a long waiting list for membership and a very strict admission policy at the door.)

But many of the so-called clubs will make you a member on the spot, and they are particularly lenient in dealing with foreigners. At the gambling clubs, there is an enforced, 48-hour waiting period (to protect you from getting drunk and impetuously gambling away your fortune, though of course you can still do that 48 hours later), so if you are interested in gaming, you have to plan ahead.

These places are constantly falling in and out of favor. And, in these times of economic difficulty, they are forever opening and closing their doors. But what follows is a current selection, in 2 categories; *nightclubs*, as used in the American sense of the term, including gambling as noted, and then *discotheques*, which, though they may have food, are primarily for fast dancing, with reliably ear-shattering, recorded music. Often the 2 categories overlap. You can usually eat at most of these places, but that is not primarily what people go to them for.

The following clubs are usually open daily, except Sunday, unless noted.

Nightclubs

Bristol Suite 14 Bruton Place, W1; 499-1938. A friendly, music lounge bar with hostesses. Open until 3. Closed weekends.

Capannina 21 Bateman Street, W1; 437-0169. A dance band and belly dancers; with French and Italian cuisine. Open until 4.

Charles Chester Casino 12 Archer Street; 734-0255. Snappy modern nightclub with gambling too. Open until 4.

Clermont Club 44 Berkeley Square, W1; 493-5587. Upstairs from Annabel's. Very select and very expensive. Excellent food. Gambling. Open until 4.

Dial 9 34–40 Great Cumberland Place, W1; 723-9245. Under the Montcalm Hotel. Very restricted membership. Open until 3.

Director's Lodge 13 Mason's Yard, Duke Street, SW1; 839-6109. Dance band and singer. Friendly and discreet hostesses. Open until 3. Closed weekends.

El Nil 17 New Bond Street, W1; 493-0855. Dancers and singers put on a lively show. Open until 3.

Embassy Club 7 Old Bond Street, W1; 499-5974. Restaurant, bar, and nightclub that goes all day long and until 4 in the morning. Very lively. Difficult and expensive to join.

Gardens 99 Kensington High Street, W8; 937-7994. Formerly Regine's, this is a glamorous rooftop setting with a garden. Very snappy and hard to get into. Open until 3.

Golden Horseshoe 3–4 Archer Street, W1; 437-5036. A bar with music on 2 floors. Open until 4. Saturday to 3 A.M.

Golden Nugget 22–32 Shaftesbury Avenue, W1; 734-6211. A huge place with several bars and red and gold decor near Piccadilly Circus. Open until 4. Saturday till 3.

Knightsbridge Sporting Club 163 Knightsbridge, SW7; 584-4252. Gambling in a friendly atmosphere. Open until 4.

Miranda 9 Kingly Street, W1; 437-6695. Red velvet and plush, big basement club with a 3-piece band, cabaret, strip-tease and hostesses. Open until 3. Closed weekends.

Maunkberry's 57 Jermyn Street, W1; 499-4623. Chic and sophisticated nightclub on a fashionable shopping street. Open until 3.

New Georgian Club 4 Mill Street, W1; 629-2042. Cabaret twice a night and bar with hostesses. Open until 1:30. Closed weekends.

Playboy Club 45 Park Lane, W1; 629-6666. Recently reopened. Lively and modern in the style that Playboy has made familiar in America. Bunnies and gambling. Open until 4. Saturday till 3.

Stringfellows 16–19 Upper St. Martin's Lane, WC2; 240-5534. Spot the celebrity, if you can, via mirrored walls which create pulsating coloured lights and reveal black suede walls. Very trendy. Open to 1:30. Disco to 3.

Wedgies 107 King's Road, SW3; 351-3461. This chic club attracts a very prestigious clientele. South American band; sometimes cabaret acts and live groups. Open till 2:30.

Discotheques and Rock Clubs

Cafe des Artistes 266 Fulham Road, SW10; 352-6200. One of the oldest established discos in town. Very popular and lively basement disco with open-door policy. Open until 2.

Chic Plaza Hotel, 42 Princes Square, W2; 229-1292. Dark and roomy basement disco. Lively. Open from 8–2.

Dingwalls Camden Lock, Chalk Farm Road, NW1;

267-4967. Club by Regent's Canal, this was once a stable for barge horses. Very lively. Open until 2. Sundays until 11.

Disco Rocco 1 Broadhurst Gardens, NW6; 328-0928. Mainly Continental. A large place with resident D.J. Every night 9:30–3.

Electric Ballroom 184 Camden High Street, NW1; 485-9006. If you fancy a jive, rock 'n roll, new wave, this is the place to go. Fun crowd for over-18s. Roller disco on Wednesdays. Fridays and Saturdays 7–midnight. Three bars.

Foubert's Foubert's Place, Carnaby Street, W1; 734-3630. Three bars and an informal atmosphere. Very, very lively. Open until 3.

Gullivers Club 11 Down Street, W1; 499-0760. American soul music is the favorite here, with live entertainment on Wednesdays. Open 9–3.

Hombre de Bahia 78 Wells Street, W1; 580-2881. Restaurant, three bars, and a band. Open 9:30–3:30. Sundays to midnight.

Legends 29 Old Burlington Street, W1; 437-9933. Trendy discotheque with circular bar. Good restaurant upstairs. Disco open from 9–2.

Marquee 90 Wardour Street, W1; 437-6603. One of the original rock clubs in London (The Rolling Stones used to play there), the Marquee features new wave and modern music. Open until 11.

Maximus Leicester Square, W1; 734-4111. Frequented mostly by tourists, so you may bump into some friends! Two bars. Open 8:30–2. Friday and Saturday to 3.

Reflections 22 Praed Street, W2; 262-7952. Mirrors everywhere, this is a lively, spacious and spectacularly lit disco for the over-21s. Open Wednesday–Saturday, 9:30–2.

Samantha's 3 New Burlington Street, W1; 734-5425. An old established, very popular split-level disco. The DJ operates from the body of an E-type Jag. Popular with groups. Open 9–3, Saturdays till 4, Sundays till 1:30.

Tingles London Tara Hotel, Scarsdale Place, W8; 937-7211. Polynesian food, burgers and snacks, in a lively disco with an extensive cocktail bar. Open 5–2, Sundays to 11:30.

Tramp 40 Jermyn Street, SW1; 734-3174. A very exclusive disco favored by the young and wealthy, and much featured in the gossip columns. Open 10:30–4.

OPERA

See MUSIC, OPERA, & DANCE.

PARKS

London's parks are among its greatest assets: wide-ranging, open, friendly, and well-maintained. And they are also quite safe, even at night. Each park has its special character. Here is an outline.

Alexandra Park and Palace N22; 883-0809. In the northern suburbs. Two hundred acres, including roller-skating rink, boating pool, and artificial ski slope. In the middle is Alexandra Palace, which was built in 1878, and used during the First World War for Belgian refugees. Band concerts and concerts for children are now performed there. Open all the time.

Battersea Park SW11; 228-2798. On the south bank of the Thames, just across the bridge from Chelsea. It has a boating pond, roller-skating areas, and beautiful gardens. Closed after dusk.

Blackheath SE3; 858-1692. Nearly 300 acres of open grassland, ideal for kite-flying or watching the sunset. Open all the time.

Bostall Heath SE2; 311-1674. Woods and open meadows. Excellent views of London and of the docks. Closes at dusk.

Clissold Park N16; 800-1021. Formerly a private estate, its 55 acres are now used for fishing, croquet, and rose gardens. Closes at dusk.

Crystal Palace SE19; 778-7148. On the summit of a steep hill, with good views in all directions. Elaborate sporting facilities (see SPORTS AND SPORTING EVENTS), and huge models of prehistoric animals, including dinosaurs (see CHILDREN'S LONDON). Closes at dusk.

Dulwich Park SE21; 693-5737. Famous for its rhododendrons and azaleas. Also, boating lake and tennis courts. Closes at dusk.

Eltham Park SE9; 850-2031. Woodland as well as open spaces, with a duck pond and striking views of central London. Open all the time.

Epping Forest Essex. One of the really great parks,

this is 6,000 acres of unspoiled forest, stretching over 6 miles, from Epping to Chingford. Wonderful walking through the oak and beech trees, and the feeling of complete solitude is easy to find, especially in the winter.

Finsbury Park N4; 263-5001. Fun fairs held here, as well as soccer, cricket, fishing, bowling, and tennis. Also a good many trees. Fun fairs in the spring and summer. Closes at dusk.

Green Park SW1. A splendid little park between Piccadilly and Buckingham Palace. Worth a detour on any stroll through central London.

Greenwich Park SE10; 858-2608. A pleasant, open park of 200 acres sloping down from the Royal Observatory to the Thames. Many fine trees. In the summer, military brass bands perform concerts. Closes at dusk.

Hampstead Heath NW3; 458-4548. Wild and rugged, Hampstead Heath is an amazing asset, considering how accessible it is to the center of town. It has 800 acres of woods, hills, and open spaces for ball sports. Perfect for walking in any kind of weather. From the top of Parliament Hill (319 feet), there is a splendid view of central London. Ask for the three most famous pubs near the heath—The Bull & Bush, The Spaniards Inn and Jack Straw's Castle—all not too far from one another. The heath is open all the time. Advisable *not* to walk there when it is dark.

Hampton Court See EXCURSIONS.

Holland Park W8; 602-2226. Centrally situated between Notting Hill and Kensington High Street, Holland Park is a peaceful oasis, its open-air theater has opera, ballet, and modern dance and drama, in the summer. Fifty-five acres of lawns and gardens, some wildlife, and peacocks.

Hyde Park W1; 262-5484. The most famous of them all. A royal park since 1536, Hyde Park was once a forest in which King Henry VIII hunted wild boar. It's much tamer now, but the threats and curses still fly every Sunday morning at Speaker's Corner, across from Marble Arch, where you can stand on a soapbox and preach away on anything at all. The Serpentine, a lake in the middle, is good for angling and cruising in a rented rowboat, and there is a good cafeteria right beside it. To many Londoners, Hyde Park, together with Kensington Gardens which is adjacent to it on the west, is one of the nicest features of London. Just for interest's sake, there were public executions held at Tyburn Gallows, near Marble Arch, until 1783. However, don't miss the park. Closes at midnight.

Kensington Gardens W8; 937-4848. More formal and elegant than Hyde Park, this was once simply the gardens of Kensington Palace (see ROYAL LONDON). You can see William III's palace, Queen Anne's Orangery and the 'Sunken Garden'. The Round Pond is alive with model boats on pleasant Sundays, and its beautifully planted flower gardens quickly make you forget the big, big city pressing close around. Closes at dusk.

Kew Gardens Kew, Surrey; 940-1171. Formally known as the Royal Botanic Gardens, this park has a splendid 300 acres of beautiful flowers, with thousands of different kinds of flowers and trees, a lake, an aquatic garden, a pagoda, and a magnificent curved glass palm house and temperate house. There are hothouses for the exotic flowers and trees, and carefully tended beds for the local varieties. Closes at dusk.

Primrose Hill NW8; 486-7905. A small park that is really just a very steep, grassy hill. From the top (200 feet high) you get good views of London. Open all the time. Probably safer to walk there at night than it is at Hampstead Heath, but take care.

Regent's Park NW1; 935-1537. Another of the really great parks, this one was laid out by Nash in the early 19th century, and named for the Prince Regent, who was going to build a country home there. Roughly circular in shape, it comprises 470 acres, much of it playing fields. There is also a splendid zoo (see CHILDREN'S LONDON), and a lake, with rowboats for rent. Winfield House, the stately official residence of the American Ambassador to Britain, is tucked into one corner of the park, but you do not see much of it through the bushes and trees. Closes at dusk.

Richmond Park Surrey; 940-0654. A magnificent and unspoiled park of 2,500 acres, just south of the river. It was first enclosed as a hunting ground by King Charles I in 1637, and has been home to badgers and weasels, and even the odd fox. Splendid views down the Thames valley. There is also golf, riding, polo and football. Closes at dusk.

St. James's Park SW1; 930-1793. A wonderful park surrounded by government buildings. A very good duck pond, crossed by a bridge, and beautiful flowers, as well as a Chinese-style lake. Good views of Buckingham Palace. In the summer, stirring band concerts twice a day. Open until midnight.

Victoria Embankment Gardens WC2. A little corner of green on the river, it is much loved by lunchtime picnickers from nearby offices. (The branch of McDonald's up by Charing Cross Station is close enough that your Big Mac will still be hot by the time you reach the park.) Its flowers in the spring and summer are beautiful to look at, and they fill the air with beautiful smells. Band concerts in the summer. Open all the time.

Victoria Park E9; 985-1957. Two-hundred seventeen acres offering a wide variety of sports, animals, historical buildings and trees. Bands play on Sunday afternoons in July and August, there is old-time dancing on Wednesdays and Saturdays in August, children's shows during the summer holidays and fun fairs during April, May and August. Open from 7 A.M. to half an hour after sunset.

Wimbledon Common SW19; 788-7655. More than 1,100 acres of heathland, with trees, open spaces, 16 miles of horse rides and a famous 19th-century windmill. Open all the time.

PASTRIES

see BAKERIES AND PASTRY SHOPS.

PERFUMES AND TOILETRIES

Chanel 76 Jermyn Street, SW1; 930-1030. The classic French perfume manufacturer.

Mary Chess 7 Shepherd Market, W1; 629-5152. High-style perfumes and other toiletries.

Penhaligon's 41 Wellington Street, WC2; 836-2150. Handmade fragrances and glamorous, expensive perfumes and toilet water.

Trumper's 9 Curzon Street, W1; 499-1850. A grand, old-fashioned barber shop that has been selling its own-make men's toiletries for a century.

PLAYGROUNDS

See CHILDREN'S LONDON.

PUBS

Ah yes, the pubs. Surely one of the great joys of Britain, the pub (or public house, to use the formal—and never used—term) is much more than just a bar. It is a social center and clubhouse, usually very closely attached to the neighborhood it is in, and there are 7,000 of them in London. Usually, you can get something to eat in a pub, often quite a respectable "pub lunch," as it is called, of something like sausage, salad, cheese or pâté, with a hot dish or two. Women can enter pubs unescorted and feel entirely comfortable, and the pub is the most likely place for a stranger to fall into conversation with a native.

In fact, the only thing wrong with the pubs is their peculiarly restricted opening hours, usually 11–3 and 5:30–11 (Sundays 12–2 and 7:30–10:30). If you want to drink later than that, see NIGHTLIFE. Children are not normally admitted into pubs, unless they have gardens or separate family rooms. Anywhere you happen to be, there are several pubs within walking distance, and one of them could easily, after a bit of exploration on foot, become your "local," as they say. To help you out, here is a selective list of favorites. (See also WINE BARS.)

Anchor 1 Bankside, Southward, SE1; 407-1577. Not really a typical pub, because it is so picturesque, and quite authentically so. A rambling old riverside pub that dates back hundreds of years, with dozens of nooks and crannies on several levels. Outdoor patio overlooks the Thames.

Angel 101 Bermondsey Wall East, SE16; 237-3603. Another riverside pub with fine views of London just across the water. Samuel Pepys and Captain Cook among its customers over the years.

Anglesea Arms 15 Selwood Terrace, Onslow Gardens, SW7; 373-7960. Draws a trendy young crowd, which tends to spill out into the front courtyard, even in the winter.

Audley 41 Mount Street, W1; 499-1843. A splendidly Victorian place in the heart of swanky Mayfair. Good pub food at the bar.

Bunch of Grapes 207 Brompton Road, SW3 (about 400 yards from Harrods); 589-4944. Good home-cooked food, with an especially wide selection of salads.

Cartoonist 76 Shoe Lane, EC4; 353-2828. In the center of the newspaper district (Fleet Street) this busy pub is decorated with old cartoons. Good snacks at the bar. Outdoor tables.

Cheshire Cheese, Ye Olde 145 Fleet Street, EC4; 353-6170. A famous old place with oak tables and sawdust on the floor. Has scarcely changed in 300 years.

Denmark 102 Old Brompton Road, SW7; 373-2403. In residential South Kensington, the Denmark draws a lively crowd in the evening, and serves an unusually complete lunch.

Duke of Cumberland 235 New King's Road, SW6; 736-2777. Big, spacious, and Victorian, this pub is a popular gathering spot in the pleasant little urban village of Parson's Green.

Duke's Head 8 Lower Richmond Road, SW15; 788-2552. A pleasant riverside pub where you can take your beer and your pâté or sandwich out onto the towpath and watch the Thames flow by.

Ennismore Arms 2 Ennismore Mews, SW7; 584-0440. This cozy little place is in a charming cobbled mews near the museums in South Kensington. Good spot for a lunchtime break.

Goose & Firkin 47 Borough Road, SE1; 403-3590. David Bruce, the publican here, brews his own beer on the premises, and is said to be the only landlord in town who does. Outdoor tables in the summer.

Grenadier 18 Wilton Row, SW1; 235-3074. A well-known pub with a military motif dating from the days when it used to be frequented by officers from Wellington's army.

Hand in Hand 7 Crooked Billet, Wimbledon, SW19; 946-5720. On the south side of the Wimbledon Common, this popular pub has a separate room into which you can take children.

Hercules Pillars 18 Great Queen Street, WC2; 242-2218. Very busy at lunchtime, this cozy pub has a real Victorian feeling.

Horse & Groom 68 Heath Street, NW3; 435-3140. On a main street in the charming little village of Hampstead, the Horse & Groom has a pleasant clublike atmosphere and good food.

Kings Head & Eight Bells 50 Cheyne Walk, SW3; 352-1820. In one of the most agreeable parts of Chelsea, this Victorian pub has a relaxed atmosphere and a good cold buffet.

Ladbroke Arms 54 Ladbroke Road, W11; 727-6648. A pleasant old-fashioned pub just north of Holland Park. Especially good for Saturday lunch.

Lamb & Flag 33 Rose Street, off Garrick Street, WC2; 836-4108. It is difficult to find the Lamb & Flag, and it is often very crowded, especially at lunchtime. But it is worth the effort, especially if you like English cheeses, of which they have a great assortment.

Lord Burleigh 250 Vauxhall Bridge Road, SW1; 834-0553. An agreeable little place where the sandwiches are so big they call them doorstoppers. Near Victoria Station.

Ludgate Cellars 1 Apothecary Street, EC4; 236-6808. A fascinating and very unusual bar occupying a series of connecting cellars underneath the railway tracks. Good cold buffet, supplemented with a couple of hot dishes at lunchtime.

Old Ship 25 Upper Mall, Hammersmith, W6; 748-2593. A popular pub with a terrace overlooking the Thames, for summertime.

Paxton's Head 153 Knightsbridge, SW1; 589-6627. A big, roomy pub decorated with glass and mirrors. Good place for a lunch break from chic shopping in Knightsbridge.

Plough 42 Christ Church Road, East Sheen, SW14; 876-4533. A charming, rural pub not far from the

heart of town.
Punch & Judy The Market, 40 Covent Garden, WC2; 836-1750. A new pub in the recently restored covered market. Very attractive.
Railway Tavern 15 Liverpool Street, EC2; 283-3598. Popular with business people from the City. Closed all day Saturday and Sunday.
Red Lion 2 Duke of York Street, SW1; 930-2030. Beautiful engraved mirrors from the 19th century, and elegant chandeliers. Just north of St. James's Square.

RAILROADS
See TRANSPORTATION.

RECORDS AND TAPES

Caruso & Co. 62 New Oxford Street, WC2; 580-6155. A wide selection of top-quality classical music, including some that are quite rare.
Collets 180 Shaftesbury Avenue, WC2; 240-3969. Jazz and folk music.
Discurio 9 Shepherd Street, W1; 493-6939. Unusual imported records, and classics.
Dobell's 21 Tower Street, WC2; 240-1354. Many American imports, including jazz and blues.
Farringdon's 42 Cheapside, EC2; 248-2816. Good stocks and discounts.
Gramophone Exchange 3 Betterton Street, WC2; 836-0976. Collectors' records, especially classical.
H M V Record Store 363 Oxford Street, W1; 629-1240. Perhaps the largest stock in London.
Record and Tape Exchange 90 Goldhawk Road, W12; 749-2930. Exchanges records and has a huge stock.
W. H. Smith Have branches all over town with record departments.

TOWER OF LONDON

Virgin Megastore 14–16 Oxford Street, W1; 631-1234. Every kind of music, much of it at bargain prices. Other branches around town.

RESTAURANTS

Forget everything you ever heard about not being able to get a good meal in London. If it was ever true, it certainly is no longer. London abounds in good restaurants of every type and style, at every price, from the very top to the very bottom. As elsewhere, the restaurant business is volatile, and business failures are not infrequent. Thus, any listing quickly becomes a bit out of date, though the high quality places tend to survive any economic climate. A number of the finest restaurants in London are in hotels, and are included in their listings, rather than here. (See HOTELS). Also, the prices keep rising steeply, so the cost symbol can be only a rough guide. It signifies the average cost of a complete dinner for 2 people including wine, coffee, service, and Value Added Tax. (Lunch at the same place, even it it is the same food, is often somewhat cheaper.)

$	Under £12
$$	Between £12 and £28
$$$	Between £28 and £40
$$$$	Over £40

Restaurants are listed by general area (though for convenience the neighborhoods are not precisely defined. For example, the Mayfair and Soho section includes all of W1.) A final note: virtually every restaurant in London is closed on Christmas (like just about everything else in town), so it seemed unnecessary to repeat that in every case.

Mayfair and Soho

Anemos 34 Charlotte Street, W1; 580-5907. Informal Greek Taverna with kebabs and spicy sausages. Open 12–3, 6–10:30. Closed Sundays. ($$)

Au Jardin des Gourmets 5 Greek Street, W1; 437-1816. Smart and elegant French restaurant with art nouveau decor. Open 12:30–2:30, 6:30–11:00. Closed Sundays. ($$)

Aunties 126 Cleveland Street, W1; 387-3226. Traditional English dishes in a pleasant little restaurant. 12:30–2, 7:30–10. Closed Sundays. ($$$)

Bentley's Oyster Bar 11 Swallow Street, Piccadilly, W1; 734-4756. Oysters, lobster, sole, turbot, all very well prepared. Open 12–2:45, 6–10:30. Closed Sundays. ($$$$)

Bertorelli Bros 19 Charlotte Street, W1; 636-4174. Well-prepared food from various cuisines at this agreeable and friendly place. Open 12–2:30, 6–10. Closed Sundays. ($$)

Bistro 42 42 Crawford Street, W1; 262-6582. Simple French cooking, consistently well done, in an informal setting. 12–3, 6–12. Sundays from 6–12. ($$)

Cafe Royal Grill Room and Le Relais, 68 Regent Street, W1; 437-9090. Traditional restaurant, opulently decorated in Rococo style. All very plush and grand, with a good selection of classic French dishes. Open 12:30–3, 6–11. Sundays from 10 A.M.–11 P.M. ($$$$)

Caravan Serai 50 Paddington Street, W1; 935-1208. Afghan specialties such as lamb cooked with yoghurt. Friendly, efficient service. Other 12–3, 6–11 (till 11:30 Fridays and Saturdays). Sundays from 6–11. ($$)

Cecconi's 5 Burlington Gardens, W1; 434-1509. Chic and very fashionable Italian restaurant, full of beautiful people, and beautifully decorated. Consistently high standards in the kitchen. Open 12–2:30, 7:15–11:45. Closed weekends. ($$$$)

Chaopraya 22 St. Christopher's Place, W1; 486-0777. Stylish and authentic Thai restaurant, in a bustling new shopping mall north of Oxford Street. Open 12–3, 6:30–11. Open Saturday evening. Closed Sundays. ($$)

Chez Gerard 5 Charlotte Street, W1; 636-4975. A pleasant and simple restaurant with consistently good basic French cooking. Atmosphere is cheerful and

Restaurants

friendly. Open 12:30–2:30, 6:30–10:45. Closed Saturday lunch. Open Sunday. ($$)

Chicago Pizza Pie Factory 17 Hanover Square, W1; 629-2669. Deep-dish pizzas served in a recreated Chicago, with Mayor Daley posters, gangster memorabilia (the Bloody Mary is called "St. Valentine's Day Massacre"), and a popular Chicago radio station (taped) in the background. Their garlic mushrooms must definitely not be missed. Serves continuously from 11:45–11:30. Sundays from 12–10:30 P.M. ($$)

Chicago Rib Shack 1 Raphael Street, SW7; 581-5595. Wondrous barbeques serving even more wondrous onion loaves, potato skins and salads. Open daily from 11:45–11:30. Sundays till 11. ($$)

Cypriana Kebab House 11 Rathbone Street, W1; 636-1057. Greek and Cypriot food served in a simple, friendly atmosphere. Open 12–2:30, 6–11. Closed Saturday lunch and all day Sunday. ($)

Equatorial 37 Old Compton Street, W1; 437-6112. Singapore cooking, a subtle and interesting blend of hot, spicy, and sophisticated, delicate flavors. Open 12–3:00, 6–11:30. Saturdays and Sundays, open all day long. ($$)

Estoril da Luigi e Fiorello 3 Denman Street, W1; 437-8700. A cozy and colorful Italian restaurant with a wide range of excellently prepared dishes. Excellent home-made pasta dishes such as spaghetti vongole; also good steaks and chops. Open 12–2:30, 6–11. Sundays till 10. ($$$)

Fuji 36 Brewer Street, W1; 734-0957. Classic Japanese cooking, including sukiyaki, tempura, and teriyaki. Calm, unhurried atmosphere recalls the mood of Japan. Open 12:30–2:30, 6–10:45. Saturdays and Sundays dinner only till 10:15. ($$$)

Gallant 5 Macclesfield Street, W1; 437-2930. Cantonese food in a bright, cheerful atmosphere. One of the best of the restaurants clustered together here in Chinatown. Duck and pork particularly recommended. Open 12 noon to 11:30 P.M. ($$)

Gay Hussar 2 Greek Street, W1; 437-0973. Long established and very popular Soho restaurant specializing in Hungarian food, but with a lot of other choices too. Bright and friendly. Open 12:30–2:30, 5:30–10:30. Closed Sundays. ($$$)

Gaylord 79 Mortimer Street, W1; 636-0808. Reliable and authentic Indian food in elegant surroundings.

North Indian tandoori favorites and the spicier fare of South India as well. Open 12–3, 6–11:30. Open Sundays till 11 P.M. ($$)

Greenhouse 27A Hays Mews, W1; 499-3331. A very stylish place that creates the air of a garden even indoors, green and cool. It has an imaginative, changing menu. Grilled meats and roasts are especially good, as well as such specialties as leek soup. Open 12–2:30, 7:30–11. Closed Saturday lunch and all day Sundays. ($$$)

Guinea Grill 30 Bruton Place, W1; 629-5613. An informal and friendly restaurant in the back of a pub. You choose from among a range of very good raw materials, steaks and chops and such. Open 12:30–2:30, 7–11. Closed Saturday lunch and all day Sunday. ($$$)

Hard Rock Cafe 150 Old Park Lane, W1; 629-0382. Very, very loud music and very good hamburgers. Popular with the young, who line up outside even in the rain. Open noon–midnight. ($$)

Hellenic 30 Thayer Street, W1; 935-1257. Authentic Greek specialties in a pleasant, friendly atmosphere. Open 12–3, 6:30–11. Closed Sundays. ($$)

Ikeda 30 Brook Street, W1; 629-2730. A tiny and well-run Japanese restaurant with an innovative menu. Mr. Ikeda cooks behind a bar counter, in plain sight of the diners, which is fun and interesting. Open 12–2:30, 6:30–10:30. Closed Sunday lunch and all day Saturday. ($$$)

Justin de Blank 54 Duke Street, W1; 629-3174. Very attractive self-service restaurant. Home-made bread, casseroles, roasts, quiches and savory pies. Open till 9 P.M. Dinner on Saturdays, but closed Sundays. ($)

Kaya 22 Dean Street, W1; 437-6630. Elegant Korean restaurant. The set meals, which offer a little of a lot of different things, are a good idea for the novice. Open 12–3, 6–11. Closed Saturday lunch and all day Sunday. ($$$)

La Cucaracha 12–13 Greek Street, W1; 734-2253. A Mexican restaurant decorated à la hacienda style, and serving typical Mexican food—burritos, enchiladas, baked and stuffed avocado Mexicano with crabmeat. There is a guitarist in the evening. Open until 11:30. Closed Saturday for dinner, and Sundays all day. ($$)

Langan's Bistro 26 Devonshire Street, W1; 935-4531. A simple and busy bistro-type restaurant with a short menu of well-prepared dishes. Open 12:30–2:15, 7–

11:30. Closed Saturday lunch and all day Sunday. ($$$)

Langan's Brasserie 1 Stratton Street, W1; 493-6437. The better-known of the 2 Langan's restaurants, this brasserie is very popular among the beautiful people of London, and those who aspire to the rank. Bustling and a bit noisy, Langan's is frequented by celebrities, and you might well spot a famous face. Open 12:30–2:30, 7–11:30. Closed Saturday lunch and all day Sunday. ($$$)

L'Artiste Muscle 1 Shepherd Market, W1; 493-6150. Comfortable and friendly wine bar, with good pâtés, quiches, and salads. Open 12–2:45, 5:30–11:30. Closed Sunday lunch. ($$)

La Pavona 5 Blandford Street, W1; 486-9696. Elegant Italian restaurant particularly strong on seafood, such as sole in vermouth sauce. Also good meat and pasta dishes. Open 12–3, 6:30–11:15. Closed Saturday lunch and all day Sunday. ($$$)

L'Escargot 48 Greek Street, W1; 437-2679. An elegant and stylish French restaurant with good English dishes too, such as dover sole and venison. Pleasant 1930s atmosphere. Open 12:15–2:30, 6:30–11:15. Closed Saturday lunch and all day Sunday. ($$$)

Le Gavroche 43 Upper Brook Street, W1; 408-0881. One of London's best (and most expensive) restaurants, in a new location. Classic French cuisine, with an imaginative touch has made this restaurant famous all over Britain. But two people will have trouble getting away for less than £80–£90. Open 12–2, 7–11. Closed Saturdays and Sundays. ($$$$)

Legends 29 Old Burlington Street, W1; 437-9933. A strikingly elegant restaurant, interestingly decorated with mirrors and potted plants. Good simple food, such as duck, steaks and fish. Open 12:30–2:30, 8:30–1:30. Closed Sundays. ($$$)

Le Petit Montmartre 15 Marylebone Lane, W1; 935-9226. Intimate and friendly French restaurant. No great imagination in the menu, but the preparation is good. Open 12–2:30, 6–11. Closed Saturday lunch and all day Sunday. ($$$)

Masako 6 St. Christopher's Place, W1; 935-1579. Rather expensive for a simple Japanese restaurant, but the food is indeed very good. All the classic dishes, such as teriyaki and sukiyaki, with a very complete, and less expensive, sushi bar in the basement. Open

12–2, 6–10. Closed Sundays. ($$$$)
Melati 21 Great Windmill Street, W1; 437-2745 and 31 Peter Street, W1; 437-2011. Both are small, pleasant restaurants offering good Southeast Asian cooking in an unpretentious way. A good range of rice and noodle dishes, and meat in spicy sauce. Open 12 noon–11:30 P.M., seven days a week.
Mirabelle 56 Curzon Street, W1; 499-4636. This is certainly one of the most elegant and luxurious restaurants in London, with some of the best food. But it is oddly controversial, and there are many Londoners who hate it. The usual reason is having been snubbed by the super-snooty staff, who tend to care most about the rich and the titled. Open 1–2:15, 7–10:45. Closed on Sundays. ($$$$)
Nanten Yakitori 6 Blandford Street, W1; 935-6219. Good Japanese cooking, in a pleasant atmosphere. If you sit at Yakitori Bar, prices are cheaper. Open 11–3, 6–10. Closed Saturday lunch and all day Sunday. ($$$)
Odin's 27 Devonshire Street, W1; 935-7296. The very finest food, in a super-elegant atmosphere, with oil paintings on the wall, and crisp linens everywhere in abundance. First-class and luxurious, with imaginative menu of classical dishes and simple English fare. Open 12:30–2:30, 7–11:30. Closed Saturday lunch and all day Sunday. ($$$$)
St. Moritz 161 Wardour Street, W1; 734-3324. Good variety of traditional Swiss dishes at this friendly, Tyrolean-style restaurant. Fondues are very good and so are the sweets, prepared on the premises. Open 12–3, 6–11:30. Closed Saturday lunch and all day Sunday. ($$)
Swiss Centre 2 New Coventry Street, W1; 734-1291. Agreeable Swiss cooking, with a very good wine list. Chowder, dumplings, and sweets all quite presentable. Open 12–2:30, 6–12. ($$$)
Tiberio 22 Queen Street, W1; 629-3561. An elegant basement restaurant, with a sophisticated clientele, Tiberio does a good job with classical Italian dishes. Open 12–3, 7–2 A.M. Closed Saturday lunch and all day Sunday. ($$$$)
Topo Gigio 46 Brewer Street, W1; 437-8516. Enjoyable and simple Italian meals in an informal basement room. Friendly serivce. Serves continuously from noon to 11:30. ($$)

Restaurants

Trader Vic's Hilton Hotel, Park Lane, W1; 493-7586. Just like its Polynesian brothers all over the world, with the familiar bamboo decor. Very popular. Open 12–3, 6:30–11:30. Closed Saturday lunch. Open Sundays. ($$$$)

Uema 160 New Cavendish Street, W1; 580-5607. Simple restaurant serving such old Indian favorites as tandoori chicken and curry. Open 12–3, 6–12. Closed Sunday lunch.

Vasco & Piero's Pavilion Academy Cinema, Poland Street, W1; 437-8774. Simple Italian cooking in a pleasant, unhurried atmosphere. Veal dishes are especially good. Open 12–3, 6–11. Closed Saturday lunch and all day Sunday. ($$$)

Verbanella 35 Blandford Street, W1; 935-2174. A bustling Italian trattoria serving simple, well-prepared dishes. Open 12–3, 5:30–11:30. Closed Sundays. ($$)

White Tower 1 Percy Street, W1; 636-8141. A friendly and authentic Greek restaurant, with all the old favorites, such as kebabs and taramasalata. Also, some imaginative and unusual dishes, all well prepared. Open 12:30–2:30, 6:30–10:30. Closed Saturdays and Sundays. ($$$)

Southwest London

A l'Ecu de France 111 Jermyn Street, SW1; 930-2837. Elegant restaurant with dark paneling and mirrored decor, and good French food stylishly prepared and served. Open 12:30–2:30, 6:30–11:15. Closed Saturday and Sunday at lunchtime. ($$$$)

Alonso's 32 Queenstown Road, SW8; 720-5986. Beautiful, sophisticated restaurant with imaginative, well-cooked food. Camembert soup, delicately prepared lamb cutlets. Open 12:30–2:30, 7:30–11:30. Closed at lunchtime Saturday and all day on Sunday. ($$$)

Bagatelle 5 Langton Street, SW10; 351-4185. A small, intimate place elegantly decorated in art deco style. Very good classic French cooking. Open 12–2, 7–11. Closed Sundays. ($$)

Barbarella 428 Fulham Road, SW6; 385-9434. Part discotheque, part restaurant, this lively place serves good and imaginative Italian food. Dinner only, 8–1 (till 2 on Saturday night). Closed Sundays. ($$$)

Brasserie St. Quentin 243 Brompton Road, SW3; 589-8005. Very trendy French restaurant popular with the fashionable young and nearly young. Good simple French food. Lively and noisy. Open 12–3 (till 4 on weekends), dinner 7–12. ($$$)

Brinkley's 47 Hollywood Road, SW10; 351-1683. Very attractive restaurant with good, well-prepared food made from the best ingredients. Smoked salmon mousse a specialty. Dinner every evening except Sunday, 7:30–11:30. ($$$)

Carlo's Place 855 Fulham Road, SW6; 736-4507. A cheerful bistro, popular in the neighborhood. The short menu changes frequently and dishes are well prepared. Attractive atmosphere. Open 12–3, 7–11:30. Closed Saturday lunch and Sundays. ($$$)

Chanterelle 119 Old Brompton Road, SW7; 373-7390. Very charming little place, though perhaps a bit precious. Simple, good French cooking. Open 12–2:30, 7–11:30, seven days a week. ($$)

Chez Nico 129 Queenstown Road, SW8; 720-6960. Classic French food prepared with great style and knowledge, and served with finesse. Makes an art out of dishes such as chicken breast stuffed with foie gras and covered in wild mushroom sauce. Dignified, sophisticated atmosphere. 12:15–1:45, 7–10:45. Lunches Tuesday–Friday, dinners Monday–Saturday. Closed Sundays. ($$$$)

Cohen & Wong's 39 Panton Street, SW1; 839-6876. The only restaurant in town where Jewish and Chinese food is offered, plus cocktails. The choice is varied. Worth a visit if only to admire the artifacts and lounge against the enormous brass bar. Open till 1 A.M. ($$)

Como Lario 22 Holbein Place, Pimlico Road, SW1; 730-2954. A bright and simple trattoria type place with a good range of Italian dishes. Open 12:15–2:30, 6:30–11:30. Closed Sundays. ($$)

Dan's 119 Sydney Street, SW3; 352-2718. A well-run and attractive place with a garden for good weather. An interesting range of well-prepared dishes, including traditional English fare. Open 12:30–2:15, 7:30–11:15. Closed Sunday evening. ($$$)

Daphne's 112 Draycott Avenue, SW3; 589-4257. Very stylish and very popular. Elegant decor and excellent food, imaginatively prepared and beautifully served. Dinner only 7:30–12. Closed Sundays. ($$$)

Restaurants

Eatons 49 Elizabeth Street, SW1; 730-0074. A stylish little place with good simple food, including traditional English dishes, well prepared. Friendly atmosphere. Open 12-2, 7–11:15. Closed Saturdays and Sundays. ($$$)

Eleven Park Walk 11 Park Walk, SW10; 352-3449. A very smart basement serving a wide variety of good Italian food. Precisely at 9, the beautiful people arrive in numbers. It is fun to get there a bit earlier and watch. Open 12:45–3, 7–12. Closed Sundays. ($$$)

English House 3 Milner Street, SW3; 584-3002. Good English dishes elegantly served in a lovely old townhouse. Open 12:30–2:30, 7:30–11:30. ($$$)

Gavvers 61 Lower Sloane Street, SW1; 730-5983. Stylish brasserie in the premises vacated by the elegant Gavroche (see *Mayfair*). Short menu of good French dishes, served in a pleasant informal mood. Dinner only, 7–11. Closed Sundays. ($$$)

Golden Duck 6 Hollywood Road, SW10; 352-3500. Sichuan and Peking food in 2 brightly decorated rooms. Duck a specialty, as you might guess from the name. Lunch Saturday and Sunday only, 1–3. Dinner every evening from 7–12. ($$$)

Gondoliere 3 Gloucester Road, SW7; 584-8062. Ornate Italian restaurant with very good pasta dishes and well-prepared vegetables. Open 12–2:30, 6–11. Closed Saturday lunch and all day Sunday ($$)

Good Earth 91 King's Road, SW3; 352-9231. Pleasant little place with good range of Cantonese and Peking dishes served by friendly waiters. Open 12:30 P.M. to 11:45. (Sundays till 11). ($$$)

Gran Paradiso 52 Wilton Road, SW1; 828-5818. Broad range of dishes, most of them classical Italian, in an attractive room hung with paintings. Open 12:30–2:30, 6:30–11:30. Closed Saturday lunchtime and all day Sunday.

Hungry Horse 196 Fulham Road, SW10; 352-7757. Good English dishes, such as lamb and puddings, in an informal and friendly bistro-type atmosphere. Open 12:30–2:30, 6:30–12. Closed lunchtime Saturday. ($$$)

Jack's Place 12 York Road, SW11; 228-8519. Friendly, informal restaurant, in which the menu changes daily, according to the availability of fresh raw materials. Good meats and fish. Open 12:30, 6:30–11. Closed lunchtime Saturday, all day Sunday and Monday. ($$)

Ken Lo's Memories of China 67 Ebury Street, SW1; 730-7734. A really wonderful Chinese restaurant, elegantly furnished and capably managed. Most areas of China are represented on the imaginative and complete menu, including Canton, Peking, Sichuan, and Shanghai. Open 12–2:30, 7–11. Closed Sundays. ($$$$)

Kudan 3 Horseferry Road, SW1; 834-3434. A sophisticated and elegant Indian/Pakistani restaurant, serving very good tandoori food. All the standard tikkas and nans, and good vegetables. Open 12–3, 7–12:30. Closed Sundays. ($$$)

La Croisette 168 Ifield Road, SW10; 373-3694. Excellent and innovative fish dishes as well as all the old favorites from the sea. Open 1–2:30, 7:30–11:30. Closed Tuesday lunchtime and all day Monday. ($$$$)

La Famiglia 7 Langton Street, SW10; 351-0761. Homemade pasta and other Italian delights in this pleasant and informal trattoria. Very friendly atmosphere. Open 12–3, 7–12. ($$)

Lafayette 32 King Street, SW1; 930-1131. Good French food, plus some American dishes, like clam chowder, in an elegant setting near St. James's. Open 12:15–2:30, 6:30–11:30. Closed Saturdays and Sundays. ($$$)

La Tante Claire 68 Royal Hospital Road, SW3; 352-6045. Very grand, very elegant, and very good. Haute cuisine of the very highest standard. Classic French dishes plus some unusual ones created on the premises. One of the best restaurants in London. Open 12:30–2, 7–11. Closed Saturdays and Sundays. ($$$$)

Le Suquet 104 Draycott Avenue, SW3; 581-1785. This is one of the best fish restaurants in London, with the pleasant atmosphere of the French Riviera. A wide range of seafood, expertly prepared. Open 12:30–2:30, 7:30–11:30. Closed at lunchtime Tuesday, all day on Monday. ($$$$)

Ma Cuisine 113 Walton Street, SW3; 584-7585. One of the very best French restaurants in London, without the forbidding atmosphere of the others. Although it is friendly and relaxed, Guy Mouillron, the chef and patron, takes his food quite seriously, and it shows. It's a tiny place and extremely popular, so you have to book your table far in advance. Open 12:30–2, 7:30–11. Closed Saturdays and Sundays ($$$$)

Restaurants

Menage à Trois 14–15 Beauchamp Place, SW3; 589-9350. A very upmarket restaurant where the middle course is left out. So you can dine on starters and desserts. A mouth-watering treat. Open till 12:15 A.M. ($$$)

Meridiana 169 Fulham Road, SW3; 589-8815. Snappy and modern Italian place with cheerful atmosphere and good food. It has a patio, for when the weather is nice. Open 12:30-3, 7–12. ($$$)

Mes Amis 31 Basil Street, SW3; 584-4484. A simple and attractive little restaurant near Harrods. All the standard French dishes, well prepared and properly served. Open 12:15–2:30 and 7:15–11. ($$$$)

Mimmo d'Ischia 61 Elizabeth Street, SW1; 730-5406. Lively Italian restaurant with some unusual veal dishes. Open 12:30–3, 7:30–11. Closed Sundays. ($$$)

Montpeliano 13 Montpelier Street, SW7; 589-0032. Friendly and very popular little Italian place, with a steady clientele. They make good use of such seasonal raw materials as pheasant. Also good pasta. Open 12:30–3, 7–12. Closed Sundays. ($$$)

Newports Knightsbridge Green, 22 Brompton Road, SW1; 589-8772. A fashionable little place with a short menu of good basic French and English dishes. Good desserts too. Open 12–3, 7–11:30. Closed Sundays. ($$)

Overton's 4 Victoria Buildings, Terminus Place, SW1; 834-3774. A fish restaurant with an elegant, but friendly atmosphere that feels somewhat like a club. The seafood is selected carefully from the markets, and cooked just right. Open till 10:30. Closed on Sundays. ($$$)

Paper Tiger 10 Exhibition Road, SW7; 584-3737. Busy, bustling basement restaurant specializing in the fiery Sichuan cuisine. The milder flavors of Peking also available, and both are very good. Lunch on Saturdays and Sundays only, 12–2:30. Dinner every night from 7–1 A.M. ($$)

Poissonerie d l'Avenue 82 Sloane Avenue, SW3; 589-2457. Seafood according to the season, well prepared. Imaginative dishes such as monkfish with Pernod, plus more standard sole and oysters. Open 12:30–3, 7–11:30. Closed Sundays. ($$$)

Pomegranates 94 Grosvenor Road, SW1; 828-6560. A quiet and comfortable basement restaurant with an unusual menu featuring dishes from all over the world. Specialties include Balinese chicken and honey and cognac ice cream. Open 12:30–2:15, 7:30–11:15. Closed lunchtime Saturday and all day Sunday. ($$$)

Sale e Pepe 13 Pavilion Road, SW1; 235-0098. Small little Italian restaurant serving good country food. Open 12–3, 7–11:30. Closed Sundays. ($$$$)

Saloos 62 Kinnerton Street, SW1; 235-4444. An elegant Pakistani restaurant with the full range of tandoori dishes, authentically prepared. Open 12–3, 7–12. Closed Sundays. ($$$$)

San Futtilo 8 Harriet Street, SW1; 235-3969. A simple, modern Italian place with particularly good veal dishes and pasta. Open 12–2:30, 7–11. Closed all day Sunday. ($$$).

San Lorenzo Fuoriporta 38 Worple Road Mews, SW19; 946-8463. An elegant little restaurant with good pasta and other Italian specialties, well prepared. Open 12:30–3, 7–11. ($$$)

September 457 Fulham Road, SW10; 352-0206. Striking decor: the dining room surrounds a conservatory full of lush greenery, which creates a pleasant garden mood even in the dead of winter. Good beef and lamb dishes. Dinner 7:30–12. (till 11 on Sundays). ($$$)

Shezan 16 Cheval Place, SW7; 589-7918. A very elegant and stylish Pakistani restaurant with extremely good food. Tikkas, tandooris, and basmati rice, all very authentically and delicately prepared. Open 12–2:30, 7–11:30. Closed Sundays. ($$$).

Tai-Pan 8 Egerton Gardens Mews. SW3; 589-8287. Hot and spicy Hunan cooking in this agreeably elegant Chinese restaurant. Open 12–2:30, 6–11:30. ($$$$)

Tandoori of Chelsea 153 Fulham Road, SW3; 589-7617. A basement room attractively decorated with bright Indian wall hangings. Good tandoori chicken and lamb and other dishes from the north of India. Lunch, Sunday only, 12:30–3. Dinner 6:30–12:30 (till 11:30 Sundays). ($$)

Tiger Lee 251 Old Brompton Road, SW5; 370-2323. An innovative and elegant Chinese restaurant pays particularly close attention to seafood. Dinner only, 6–11:30. ($$$).

Walton's 121 Walton Street, SW3; 584-0204. One of the most elegant—and most expensive—restaurants in town. Impressively luxurious, with food that, although good, is seldom great. Open 12:30–2:30, 7:30–11:30. ($$$$)

INNS OF COURT

Wild Thyme 96 Felsham Road, SW15; 789-3323. Cheerful and crowded little bistro with an imaginative menu. Open 12–2:30, 7:30–11. Closed lunchtime Saturday and all day Sunday and Monday. ($$)

Wilton's 55 Jermyn Street, SW1; 629-9955. Plush Victorian dining room with first-class English food, from the very finest raw materials. Fish a specialty. Wonderful old-fashioned atmosphere. Open 12:30–2:30, 6:30–10:30. Closed all day Saturday and Sunday. ($$$$)

West London

Al Amir 112 Edgware Road, W2; 402-0087. Elegant Lebanese restaurant near Marble Arch. The unusual and innovative menu is certain to cause surprise, including, for example, brain salad as an hors d'oeuvre. Serves continuously from noon to midnight.

Byblos 262 Kensington High Street, W8; 603-4422. Lebanese grills and hummus, good breads in a simple but friendly restaurant. Serves continuously from noon to midnight. ($$)

Casa Porrelli 1A Launceston Place, W8; 937-6912. Lovely little restaurant with especially good pasta dishes. Friendly service. Open 12–2:30, 6–10:30. Closed Sundays. ($$).

Chez Franco 3 Hereford Road, W2; 229-5079. A small, trattoria-style Italian restaurant. Home-made pasta makes the spaghetti memorable. Open 12:30–3, 7–12. Closed Saturday lunch and all day Sunday. ($$$)

Chez Moi 3 Addison Avenue, W11; 603-8267. A small, elegant French restaurant. Service is unhurried and attentive, and the food is usually very good. Hot smoked salmon quiche is a specialty. Dinner only, 7–11:30. Closed on Sundays. ($$$)

Costas Grill 12 Hillgate Street, W8; 229-3794. Greek Cypriot cafe with good fish and casseroles. Friendly. Serves continuously from noon to 10:30. Closed on Sundays. ($)

Da Gianbruno 6 Hammersmith Broadway, W6; 748-9393. Trattoria-style restaurant with good Italian specialties, such as pasta and meat dishes. Open 12–3, 6–11:30. ($$)

Didier 5 Warwick Place, W9; 286-7484. An informal and very pleasant restaurant in a residential neigh-

Restaurants

borhood. Husband and wife team provide good, varied food and attentive service. Open 12:30–2:30, 7:30–10:30. Closed all day Saturday and all day Sunday. ($$$)

Diwana Bhel-Poori House 50 Westbourne Grove, W2; 221-0721. Delicious Indian food for very little money. Good value. Open 12–2:45, 6–10:45. ($)

Geal's Fish Restaurant 2 Farmer Street, W8; 727-7969. The very best fish and chips, served in comfort with good desserts. Open 12–3, 6–11:30. Closed Sundays and Mondays. ($)

Gino's 70 The Mall, Ealing, W5; 567-5237. Delicious assortment of simple Italian foods, such as minestrone and veal limone. Open 12–3, 6:30–11:30. ($$)

Great Mughal 2 Hyde Park Square, W2; 258-3507. Authentic tandoori cooking in what is, for an Indian restaurant, unusual elegance. The waiters are friendly and helpful toward the uninitiated, and those familiar with Indian food will find all their favorites here. Open 12–3, 6:30–11:30. ($$)

Halepi 18 Leinster Terrace, W2; 723-4097. Greek Cypriot specialities in this friendly, welcoming taverna. Good charcoal grills. Serves from noon to 1 A.M. ($)

Hung Toa 54 Queensway, W2; 727-6017. A modern and bright Chinese restaurant specializing Cantonese dishes, which are prepared faultlessly. The duck is especially good. Serves continuously from noon to 11 P.M. ($$)

I Ching 40 Earl's Court Road, W8; 937-0409. Another good Chinese restaurant with an elegant atmosphere. Cooking from various regions of China, with the chicken and pork dishes particularly good. Friendly service. Serves continuously from noon to midnight. ($$)

Kalamaras 66 Inverness Mews, W2; 727-9122. Authentic Greek cooking in this simple little place. Friendly atmosphere. Dinner only, 7–11:30. Closed Sundays. ($$$)

l'Artiste Assoiffe 122 Kensington Park Road, W11; 727-5111. A pleasant French restaurant in an old Victorian house. It has a long menu with few surprises, but a record of reliability on the familiar dishes. Lunch, Saturday only, from 12–2:45. Dinner 6:30–11. Closed on Sundays. ($$$)

La Jardiniere 149 Holland Park Avenue, W11; 221-6090. A cheerful, garden-style restaurant serving very good food such as game pie and duck. Friendly, unpretentious atmosphere. Lunch Sunday only 12:30–2:30. Dinner every day 6:30–11:45. ($$)

La Lupa 23 Connaught Street, W2; 723-0540. Simple Italian fare, well prepared and served with courtesy and style. A pleasant place. Open 12–2:30, 6:30–11:30, Sunday 6:30–11. ($$)

La Paesana 30 Uxbridge Street, W8; 229-4332. A popular Italian restaurant with homemade pasta. Open 12–3, 6:30–12. Closed Sundays. ($)

Le Chef 41 Connaught Street, W2; 262-5945. Cheery little French bistro just north of Hyde Park. Good French provincial cooking and friendly service. Open 12:30–2:30, 7:30–11:30. Closed Saturday lunch, and all day Sunday and Monday. ($$$)

Lebanese 60 Edgware Road, W2; 723-9130. For genuine Lebanese dishes in an atmosphere of mirrors, inlaid brass chairs, arches and dim lights. Open till 11:30. ($$)

Leith's 92 Kensingtom Park Road, W11; 229-4481. Very elegant restaurant, with a good menu of French-inspired dishes. A bit pricey, but it is a memorable evening out. Dinner only, 7:30–12. ($$$$)

Le Quai St. Pierre 7 Stratford Road, W8; 937-6388. Has the style of a waterfront restaurant on the French Riviera and specializes in every kind of seafood, some of it imported from France. Mussels, oysters, scallops, crab, bass, turbot, on and on and on. Very good. Open 12:30–2:30, 7:30–11:30. Closed Monday lunch and all day Sunday. ($$$$)

Mandarin Kitchen 14 Queensway, W2; 727-9012. A big and popular place, serving a wide range of Cantonese food, well prepared. Frequent daily specials made from steamed fresh fish. Serves continuously from noon to 11:30. ($$)

Mildred's 135 Kensington Church Street, W8; 727-5452. A very informal and modest restaurant that does a good job with such standards as game pie. Friendly atmosphere. Open 12–3, 6–10:30. Closed Saturday lunch and all day Sunday. ($$$)

New Leaf 35 Bond Street, Ealing, W5; 567-2343. Very good Chinese cooking in the Peking and Sichuan mode. Stylish modern interior. Open 12–2:15, 6–11:45. Closed Sunday and Monday lunch. ($$)

North China Restaurant 305 Uxbridge Road, Acton, W3; 992-9183. Colorful Peking restaurant, with duck

the specialty. Friendly family service and cheerful atmosphere. Open 12–2:30, 6–11:30. ($$)
Phoenicia 11 Abingdon Road, W8; 937-0120. Well-cooked Lebanese dishes in a pleasant, welcoming atmosphere. Serves continuously from noon to 11:45 P.M. ($$$)
Romano's 30 Clifton Road, W9; 286-2266. Friendly little trattoria with excellent homemade tortellini and good veal dishes. Open 12–3, 6–11. Closed Monday lunchtime and all day Sunday. ($$)
Salino 25 Sale Place, W2; 402-7722. Informal little place with Sicilian specialties. Simple and attractive. Open 12–3, 6–11:30. Closed Saturday lunch and all day Sunday. ($$)
Shireen 270 Uxbridge Road, W12; 749-5927. Elegant Indian restaurant specializing in tandoori dishes as well as the spicy curries from South India. Seasoning is very, very good, and the atmosphere is sophisticated. Open 12–3, 6–11:30. ($$).
Siam 12 St. Albans Grove, W8; 937-8765. Here you sit on cushions and watch graceful Thai dancers while you enjoy authentic Thai dishes, such as pork satay and subtly flavored soups. Open 12:30–2:30, 6:15–11:15. Closed lunchtime, Monday and Saturday. ($$)
Topo d'Oro 39 Uxbridge Street, W8; 727-5813. A big, friendly Italian restaurant in several basement rooms. Familiar dishes such as pasta and veal dishes are well prepared and efficiently served. Open 12–3, 6–11:30. ($$)
Trattoria Il Carretto 20 Hillgate Street, W8; 229-9988. A cozy trattoria with the atmosphere of a small town in Italy. Familiar dishes such as veal are well cooked, in delicious homemade sauces. Open 12–3, 6–12. ($$)
Wheeler's Alcove 17 Kensington High Street, W8; 937-1443. Very popular fish restaurant, with a dazzlingly long seafood menu that includes 23 different dover soles. High-quality raw materials ensure high-quality meals. Open 12–2:30, 6–11. Sundays 12:30–2:30, 7–10:15. ($$$)

Covent Garden Area

Bardigiana 5 Bernard Street, WC1; 837-8744. A friendly little trattoria offering simple Italian food. Good atmosphere. Open 12–3, 6–11. Closed on Sundays. ($$)

Boulestin 25 Southampton Street, WC2; 836-7061. One of London's finest restaurants, with an elegant sophistication that recalls a calmer, less hurried time, and superb French food in the very best tradition. The Boulestin is for a long leisurely meal with someone you love. Unforgettable. Open 12:30–2:30, 7–11:15. Closed lunchtime Saturday and all day Sunday. ($$$$)

Brasserie du Coin 54 Lamb's Conduit Street, WC1; 405–1717. A very pleasant brasserie with a jolly, cheerful atmosphere and good, simple French cooking. Very popular at lunchtime. Open 12–3, 6–10. Closed Saturday and Sunday. ($$$)

Diamond 23 Lisle Street, WC2; 437-2517. Modest little Cantonese restaurant with all your favorites—duck, spareribs, crab. Serves continuously from noon to 2:30 A.M. ($$)

Flounders 19 Tavistock Street, WC2; 836-3925. A stylish little seafood place, with a wide variety; cod, skate, sole, oysters, prawns, and anything else you can think of. Open 12:30–3, 5:30–11:30. Closed on Sundays. ($$)

Food for Thought 31 Neal Street, WC2; 836-0239. A vegetarian restaurant, with a good selection of homemade healthful food. Tisanes available to drink, or you may take your own wine.

Ganpath 372 Gray's Inn Road, WC1; 278-1938. South Indian vegetarian cooking, very spicy, very good. Open 12–3, 6–10:15. Closed Sundays. ($$)

Grange 39 King Street, WC2; 240–2939. Small and elegant restaurant with set menu that changes frequently. Mussels in cream, dover sole, venison, and baby lamb, all nicely done with style. Open 12:30–2:30, 7:30–11:30. Closed lunchtime Saturday and Sunday. ($$$)

Happy Garden 47 Charing Cross Road, WC2; 437-7472. A bright Chinese restaurant serving Cantonese specialties, many of which are not on the English-language menu (so just ask). Meals served from noon to 11. ($$$)

Il Fornello 150 Southampton Row, WC1; 837-4584. Family-run trattoria with friendly atmosphere and good food. Open 11:30 A.M. to 11 P.M. Closed Sundays. ($)

Inigo Jones 14 Garrick Street, WC2; 836-6456. A very smart and stylish restaurant, good for after the theater. Elegant service of well-prepared dishes such as poached fish, steak tartare. Open 12:30–2:30, 5:30–

11:30. Closed Saturday lunch and all day Sunday. ($$$$)

Interlude de Tabaillau 7 Bow Street, WC2; 379-6473. Very stylish and very elegant French restaurant, right by the Covent Garden opera house. Classical cooking, especially featuring a wide variety of hot mousses. Very popular. Open 12:30–2, 7–11:30. Closed lunchtime on Monday and Saturday, and all day Sunday. ($$$$)

Joe Allen 13 Exeter Street, WC2; 836-0651. Lively and crowded, like its namesake in New York. It serves American fare such as spareribs and hamburgers. Open noon–1 A.M. ($$)

Les Halles 57 Theobald's Road, WC1; 242-6761. The real feel of Paris, with marble-top tables and authentic French cuisine. All the old favorites, such as onion soup and sole meuniere. Very pleasant atmosphere. Open 12–3, 7–11. Closed Saturday lunch and Sundays. ($$$)

L. S. Grunt Pizza Company 12 Maiden Lane, WC2; 379-7722. Pizzas, chocolate cheesecake in a Chicago motif. Open noon to 11:30 P.M. Sundays till 10 P.M. ($$)

Manzi's 1 Leicester Square, WC2; 734-0224. A bustling fish restaurant, with bright tablecloths and a friendly atmosphere. They buy very good fresh fish and cook it well, to order. Very wide selection. Location makes it good for before or after the theater. Open 12–2:40, 5:30–11. Closed Sunday lunch. ($$$)

Mon Plaisir 21 Monmouth Street, WC2; 836-7243. A popular French restaurant with much of the feel of a bistro in Paris. Good, basic food, well prepared. Crowded and lively. Open 12–2, 6–11. Closed Saturdays and Sundays. ($$$)

Monte Grappa 339 Gray's Inn Road, WC1; 837-6370. A friendly trattoria, with simple, well-prepared Italian food. Meals served from 10 A.M. to midnight. ($$$)

Neal Street Restaurant 26 Neal Street, WC2; 836-8368. A stylishly decorated restaurant featuring such traditional English fare as game and lamb. Pleasant atmosphere. Open 12:30–2:30, 7:30–11. Closed Saturdays and Sundays. ($$$$)

New Rasa Sayang 3 Leicester Place, WC2; 437-4556. Southeast Asian cooking in an exotic atmosphere. Coconut flavored meats, and spicy charcoal grill. Open 12–3, 6–10:45. Saturdays and Sundays, open all day. ($$)

Poons & Co 27 Lisle Street, WC2; 437-1528. A famous old Chinese restaurant with good Cantonese cooking. Such specialties as wind-dried meat and shellfish. Busy and crowded much of the day. Continuous serving from noon to 11:30. Closed Sundays. ($$$)

Poons of Covent Garden 41 King Street, WC2; 240-1743. A much less harried and more relaxed Poons, with an elegant atmosphere and the same good Cantonese food. One of the best Chinese restaurants in town. Serves continuously from noon to 11:30 P.M. Closed on Sundays. ($$$)

Porters 17 Henrietta Street, WC2; 836-6466. Simple, good English cooking—meat and game pies and flans and such—in a friendly atmosphere. Open 12–3, 5:30–11:30. ($$)

Rules 35 Maiden Lane, WC2; 836-5314. Charles Dickens, Lily Langtry, and others loved the place, and so can you. It seems straight out of the 19th century, and is decorated with paintings and cartoons. Traditional English dishes such as Yorkshire pudding are well prepared. Open 12:15–2:45, 6–11:15. Closed Saturday lunch and Sundays. ($$$)

Simpson's-in-the-Strand 100 The Strand, WC2; 836-9112. Traditional English cooking in an elegant, men's-club atmosphere. As the waiters wheel around heated silver trolleys bearing great hunks of beef and duck and lamb, you get the feeling that it was always thus. Open 12–3, 6–9:30. Closed Sundays. ($$$)

Tagore Brunswick Centre, Bernard Street, WC1; 837-9397. Another of London's top-flight Indian restaurants, the Tagore serves a number of different cuisines, including Kashmiri, Tandoori, and curries, as well as the vegetarian thali of South India. Open 12–3, 6–11:30. Closed Sunday lunch. ($$$)

Thomas de Quincey's 36 Tavistock Street, WC2; 240-3972. A pleasant restaurant in an interesting old building, Thomas de Quincey's has a good range of standard English cooking. Service sometimes a bit vague. Open 12:30–3, 6–11. Closed lunchtime Saturdays and all day Sunday. ($$$$)

Trattoria Imperia 19 Charing Cross Road, WC2; 930-8364. A busy little Italian restaurant, with a wide selection of traditional dishes. Open 12–2:45, 6–11:25. Closed on Saturday lunch and Sundays. ($$)

Restaurants

North London

Anna's Place 90 Mildmay Park, N1; 249-9379. A friendly little restaurant, warmly decorated, with good food, especially the fish dishes. Dinner only, 7–10:30. Closed Sundays and Mondays. ($$)

Asuka 209A Baker Street, Berkeley Arcade, NW1; 486-5026. Striking Japanese restaurant starkly decorated in black and white. Good traditional fish dishes beautifully prepared. Open 12–2:30, 6–10:30. Closed Saturday lunch and all day Sunday. ($$$)

Bloom's 130 Golder's Green Road, NW11; 455-1338. Traditional kosher specialties including chopped herring and salt beef. Continuous service from noon to 9:30. Closed Friday and Saturday. ($$)

Bunny's 7 Pond Street, NW3; 435-1541. A popular and informal little French restaurant that has very good food without any pretensions. Good desserts, too. Lunch, Sunday only, 12–3. Dinner every evening except Monday, 7–11. ($$)

Capability Brown 351 West End Lane, NW6; 794-3234. Stylish little French restaurant with good food though it is wise to stick to their simplest dishes. 12:30–2:30, 7–11:30. Closed Sundays. ($$$)

Carrier's 2 Camden Passage, N1; 226-5353. An intimate and elegant restaurant in 3 rooms, Carrier's is one of the best in London, despite its somewhat remote location. Robert Carrier's imagination and skill are always at work, creating such unforgettable dishes as mussel soup and chicken breasts stuffed with truffles. Open 12:30–2:30, 7:30–11:30. Closed Sundays. ($$$$)

Chaglayan Kebab House 86 Brent Street, Hendon, NW4; 202-8575. Turkish and Greek dishes well prepared in this Cypriot restaurant, which has a happy, courteous atmosphere. Open 12–3, 6–12. Closed Sundays and Mondays. ($)

Chalcot's Bistro 49 Chalcot Road, NW1; 722-1956. Attractive little French restaurant. Good value. Open 12:30–2:30, 7–11. Closed Mondays. ($$)

Chalk & Cheese 14 Chalk Farm Road, NW1; 267-9820. Interesting range of different dishes, including crepes and fish dishes. Good value. Open 12–3, 7–11. Closed Sunday evenings, and all day Monday. ($)

Diwana Bhel-Poori House 121 Drummond Street, NW1; 387-5556. Very inexpensive Indian vegetarian food, well prepared and well served. Often extremely crowded, especially on weekends, so try to pick an off hour. Meals served continuously from noon till 10:45. Closed Mondays. ($)

Finches 250 Finchley Road, NW3; 435-8622. Good English food prepared in the traditional way, in a pleasant and friendly restaurant. Open 12–2:15, 7–11:15. Closed dinnertime Sunday and all day Monday. ($$)

Four Seasons 69 Barnsbury Street, N1; 607-0857. An agreeable little French restaurant, with a high standard of cuisine. There is a short menu, changed frequently, of interesting dishes such as turbot and snails. Open 12:30–2:30, 7–11. Closed Sundays. ($$$)

Frederick's Camden Passage, N1; 359-2888. An elegant and very popular restaurant with a French chef who changes the menu frequently. Rabbit in white wine sauce was a recent specialty. Open 12:30–2:30, 7:30–11:30. Closed Sundays. ($$$)

Gourmet Rendezvous 263 Finchley Road, NW3; 435-0755. A modest Cantonese restaurant with a good local reputation. Friendly and informal. Open 12–2:30, 6:30–12. ($$)

Green Cottage 9 New College Parade, Finchley Road, NW3; 722-5305. Another Cantonese restaurant, with a wide selection and a friendly atmosphere. Meals served from noon to 11:30 P.M.

Harry Morgan's 31 St. John's Wood High Street, NW8; 722-1869. Salt beef, chopped liver, other Kosher favorites at this pleasant little Jewish restaurant. Open 12–3, 6–10. Sunday, continuous service all day. ($)

Julius's 39 Upper Street, Islington, N1; 226-4380. Julius Oberegger prepares the food out where you can see him, and delicious it is—mushroom crepes, poached turbot, steaks. Open 12:30–2:30, 7:30–11:45. Closed Saturday lunchtime and all day Sunday. ($$)

Keats 3 Downshire Hill, NW3; 435-1499. Like eating in the house of a friend, Keats is decorated with books and paintings, and the standard of the food is excellent. Imaginative French dishes, beautifully prepared and served. Dinner only, 7–11:30. Closed Sundays. ($$$$)

Kuo Yuan 217 Willesden High Road, NW10; 459-2297. Peking duck and other duck dishes are the specialty of this bright Chinese restaurant, which is often crowded. Open 12–2:30, 6–11. ($$)

L'Aubergade 816 Finchley Road, NW11; 455-8853.

Restaurants

Very authoritative French cooking, served in a pleasant, unhurried atmosphere here in the northern suburbs. All the standard dishes, well done. Open 12–2:30, 7–11:30. Closed Saturday lunchtime, all day Sunday. ($$)

La Casalinga 64 St. John's Wood High Street, NW8; 722-5959. Pasta and other Italian dishes well prepared and well served in this popular neighborhood restaurant. Open 12–2:30, 6–11:15. Closed Sundays. ($$)

Lord's Rendezvous 24 Finchley Road, NW8; 722-4750. An unusual combination: Peking food in a former railway station. Friendly, attentive service. Open 12–2:30, 6:30–11:15. ($$$)

M'sieur Frog 31A Essex Road, N1; 226-3495. A friendly and agreeable French bistro, with good provincial food, well prepared and pleasantly served. Dinner only 7–11:30. Closed Sundays. ($$$)

Oslo Court Restaurant Prince Albert Road, NW8; 722-8795. An excellent and quite elegant restaurant overlooking Regent's Park. Food is Balkan and Greek, but with traditional English dishes as well. Open 12:30–3, 7–11. Closed Sunday evenings. ($$$)

San Carlo 2 Highgate High Street, N6; 340-5823. Lively Italian restaurant in one of London's most pleasant suburban villages. Open 12:30–3, 7–12. ($$$)

Viceroy of India 3 Glentworth Street, NW1; 486-3401. Very elegant Indian restaurant with good Tandoori food of the type enjoyed in north of the country. Looking through glass, you can see the tandoor oven at work. Open 12–3, 6:30–11:30. ($$$)

Vijay 49 Willesden Lane, NW6; 328-1087. Authentic South Indian cooking—hot spicy curries and vegetarian dishes. The atmosphere is pleasant, and Mr. Ramanthan, who presides, is welcoming. Open 12–2:45, 6–10:45 (till 11:45 Fridays and Saturdays). ($)

East London

Ashley's 10 Copthall Avenue, EC2; 638-9363. A comfortable basement restaurant with good grills and chops, and well-selected and well-prepared fresh vegetables. Friendly atmosphere. Lunch only. 12–3. Closed Saturdays and Sundays. ($$$)

Au Provencal 295 Railton Road, Herne Hill, SE24; 274-9163. Charming, informal French bistro with good, well-prepared food and a friendly atmosphere. Dinner only, 7–10:30. ($$)

Baron of Beef Gutter Lane, Gresham Street, EC2; 606-6961. An elegant and luxurious paneled restaurant serving traditional English fare, such as roasts and fish. Open 12–3, 5:30–9:30. Closed Saturdays and Sundays. ($$)

Bill Bentley's Swedeland Court, 202 Bishopsgate, EC2; 283-1763. A friendly and bustling luncheon spot especially noted for its fish. Lunch only 12–3. Closed Saturdays and Sundays. ($$$)

Bloom's 90 Whitechapel, High Street, E1; 247-6001. Very good salt beef, and other strictly kosher foods in this traditional Jewish restaurant. Friendly atmosphere. Open 11:30–9:30. Closed Friday evenings and all day Saturday. ($)

Bubb's 329 Central Market, EC1; 236-2435. A busy bistro with well-prepared French food. You need to reserve a table well in advance. Lunch only. 12:15–2. Closed Saturdays and Sundays. ($$$)

Chinatown 795 Commercial Road, Limehouse, E14; 987-2330. A busy little Cantonese restaurant in the docklands. Very popular, and reservations are essential. Serves from noon–3, 6–11. ($$)

Cotillion Room Bucklersbury House, Cannon Street, EC4; 248-4735. Formal and luxurious atmosphere much favored by financiers from the area. Traditional food, classically prepared. Lunch only, 12–3. Closed Saturdays and Sundays. ($$$$)

Good Friends 139 Salmon Lane, Stepney, E14; 987-5498. More than 2 decades of good Cantonese cooking here, a distinguished tradition. Reservations are essential, so they must still be doing something right. Meals served from 12:30–11 P.M. ($$)

Le Gamin 32 Old Bailey, EC4; 236-7931. A simple and bustling brasserie with very good provincial food. A bit too expensive, considering the atmosphere, but fun. Lunch only 12–2:30. Closed Saturdays and Sundays. ($$$)

Le Poulbot 45 Cheapside, EC2; 236-4379. Extremely elegant and plush restaurant much favored by businesspeople from the surrounding financial district. One gets the feeling that no one at the Poulbot is paying for his or her own lunch. Very good, short menu of excellently prepared French dishes. Lunch only, 12–3. Closed Saturdays and Sundays. ($$$)

Restaurants

Luigi's 129 Gipsy Hill, Dulwich, SE19; 670-1843. Sleek, modern Italian restaurant well away from the center of town, with good pasta and veal dishes. Open 12–2:30, 6:30–11:15. Closed lunchtime Saturday and all day Sunday. ($$)

National Theater Restaurant Upper Ground, South Bank, SE1; 928-2033. A pleasant restaurant in the South Bank arts complex, overlooking the Thames. You don't even have to be going to the theater to eat there. Lunch, Saturday only, 12:15–2:30. Dinner every day except Sunday 5:30–11:30 ($$)

Pyramid 78 East Dulwich Grove, SE22; 693-0372. Very simple restaurant oddly placed in a nondescript suburban street, but the food—classic French cuisine—is very, very good. Dinner only, 7–10. Closed Sundays and Mondays. ($$)

RSJ 13A Coin Street, SE1; 928-4554. Informal French bistro with good, simple food. A bargain. Open 12–2:30, 6–11:30. Closed Saturday lunch and all day Sunday. ($$)

Shares 12 Lime Street, EC3; 623-1843. Very elegant and stylish restaurant with set meals of 3 or 4 courses, beautifully prepared and served. Brunch 11:30–1. Lunch 11:30–3. Closed Saturdays and Sundays. ($$$$)

Restaurants by Type

London abounds in French, Italian, Indian/Pakistani, Chinese, and Japanese restaurants, and you'll find a goodly number listed for each region. You'll also find many restaurants listed that serve traditional English dishes such as game pies and roast meats. Below are some brief listings of specialized restaurants that might be a little more difficult to isolate in this city of restaurants.

Afghan

Caravan Serai

American

Chicago Pizza Factory

Chicago Rib Shack
Joe Allen

Greek

Anemos
Costas Grill
Cypriana
Halepi
Hellenic
Kalamaras
Oslo Court
White Tower

Hungarian

Gay Hussar

Kosher

Blooms
Cohen & Wong's
Harry Morgan's

Lebanese

Al Amir
Byblos
Lebanese
Phoenicia

Mexican

La Cucaracha

Polynesian

Pomegranates
Trader Vic's

Southeast Asian

Chaopraya
Equatorial
Kaya
Melati
New Rasa Sayang
Siam

Swiss

St. Moritz
Swiss Centre

ROYAL LONDON

Britain's much-beloved Royal Family are one of the country's greatest assets, symbolizing both the continuity of the state and the moral values of the Christian family. And despite their country palaces, their presence is much felt in London. Following are some attractions associated with the monarchy.

Buckingham Palace The residence of the Queen, it is one of the most familiar landmarks, though its connection with the monarchy is rather recent. It was built by the Duke of Buckingham in a mulberry garden given him by Queen Anne, and then extensively remodeled, at the direction of George IV, by John Nash. It became a royal residence only in 1837, when the young Queen Victoria took up residence. The palace and its 40-acre garden are never open to the public. But you can see the famous Changing of the Guard ceremony every morning just before 11:30 (every other morning in the winter).

Outside the main gate (where you watch the guard ceremony) is the gilded bronze Queen Victoria Memorial, and around the handsome plaza are ornate gray stone pillars, each carved with the name of a different imperial territory, from Malay States to Newfoundland—a reminder of how recently this spot in her Empire was, in a literal sense, the center of the world.

Around the side of the palace (to your left, as you face the main gate) is the Queen's Gallery (see MUSEUMS—ART). Walking past it, and keeping the palace on your right, you come next to the Royal Mews, where the state coaches and ceremonial horses used on occasions like Prince Charles's wedding procession in 1981 are on permanent display, Wednesday and Thursday afternoons.

Clarence House The white stone residence of Queen Elizabeth the Queen Mother, into which Lady Diana Spencer moved the day that her engagement to Prince Charles was announced in 1981. It was built in 1825 by John Nash for William IV when he was the Duke of Clarence, and restored in 1949 for Princess Elizabeth, the present queen. Not open to the public.

Horse Guards At the eastern end of St. James's Park, the Horse Guards is a building, with an ornate clock tower, that was used as a guard house for Whitehall Palace and is now a military headquarters. Countless tourists have had someone take their photograph standing next to the mounted guards of the Household Cavalry who are on duty there. (The guard is changed daily at about 11 o'clock.) A passage from the Horse Guards leads to the Horseguards Parade, a graveled space where the ceremony of Trooping the Color is performed by the Guards Brigade on the queen's official birthday, in early June.

Kensington Palace The only place on this list that is not an easy walk from The Mall, Kensington Palace is at the western edge of Kensington Gardens (see PARKS). It is the residence of, among others, Prince Charles and his wife, the former Lady Diana Spencer, and of his aunt, Princess Margaret. It was in Kensington Palace that the 18-year-old Princess Victoria was awakened by the Archbishop of Canterbury one night in 1837 with the news that she had become Queen, beginning a reign of more than 6 decades. The public can visit part of the palace, including its state apartments, which contain some grand old rooms with memorabilia of several monarchs, and costume jewelry.

HOUSES OF PARLIAMENT

Marlborough House Now the headquarters of the Commonwealth Secretariat, Marlborough House, with all its grandeur, gives a hint of the glittering court life that used to be the rule in London. In its days as the home of the glamorous young Bertie and Alex—the Prince and Princess of Wales who were married in 1863—its style was glittering indeed, in contrast to the somber life then being led by the Prince's mother, Queen Victoria, who was in deep mourning for Prince Albert. Bertie and Alex had 85 servants at Marlborough House, including 3 or 4 men who did nothing but clean the silver, and 2 others who took care of the 300 bowls of fresh flowers.

Royal Military Chapel Better known as the Guards' Chapel, this is the church of the men who guard the Queen (though it is open to anyone), on the south side of St. James's Park. It was wrecked by a bomb one Sunday morning in 1944, with the loss of 121 lives, but the original apse has been preserved within a modern reconstruction, and so, as a memorial, have some of the tattered old banners of the military units. A good place to go on a Sunday morning.

St. James's Palace This brick mansion has far more royal history than Buckingham Palace, where the Queen lives now, symbolized by the fact that foreign ambassadors to Britain are still accredited, technically, to "the court of St. James's." The palace stands at the foot of St. James's Street, next door to Clarence House, on the site of St. James's Hospital, an 11th-century home for "14 maiden lepers, living chastely and honestly." Henry VIII chose this site as a home for himself and his second wife, Anne Boleyn, a retreat from the official palace at Whitehall across the park. As we know, Anne did not get to live there for long, but St. James's has been a royal residence ever since, becoming the preeminent palace in 1698 after most of Whitehall Palace was destroyed by fire.

From a window overlooking Friary Court in St. James's, the last Prince of Wales, with Mrs. Wallis Simpson at his side, watched the ceremony at which he was proclaimed King Edward VII in 1936. One part of the palace is currently occupied by the Duke of Kent, a first cousin of the Queen, and his family. Ordinarily, it is not open to the public, but they may wander through its courtyards, and attend services in its chapels. The Queen's Chapel in St. James's is a masterpiece by Inigo Jones; the Chapel Royal (where John Donne sometimes preached) has a ceiling attributed to Holbein, and both are well worth a visit.

In the days when the monarch lived in St. James's, noblemen built their own grand houses in the neighborhood, to be close to the royal court. One of them was the first Earl Spencer, from whom Diana, the Princess of Wales, is descended. The great palladian Spencer residence he built in the 1760s is, happily, well preserved (though now offices). It is on the southwest side of St. James's Place, adjoining Green Park.

The Tower of London A fortress, former royal residence and jail, the Tower is fascinating, for young and old alike. It is also very popular, so you should try to arrive as close as possible to the 9:30 A.M. opening, to avoid the crowds, especially during school holidays and the summer. Perhaps the Tower's greatest attraction is the Jewel House, where you can see the Crown Jewels, including the Royal Scepter with its 530-carat diamond and the Imperial State Crown, made with 3,000 stones, among them a ruby that Henry V is said to have won at Agincourt. Do not be put off by the lines at the Jewel House; they move quickly and it is worth the wait.

SIGHTS WORTH SEEING
See also ROYAL LONDON

Admiralty Whitehall, SW1. Once the headquarters of the mighty British Navy (hence the name), Admiralty has become the main office of the Civil Service. It dates from 1722, and includes a handsome screen added by Adam in 1760. A large triple archway from it opens onto the Mall. The middle of the 3 arches is opened only for royalty (though some of the many thousands of Londoners who drive through one or the other every morning and evening grumble at the restriction). Over the arch is the Admiralty library.

Bank of England Threadneedle Street, EC2. A gigantic, massive fortress symbolizing London's position (even now) at the center of the financial world. It is the bank for bankers and governments, and in its bowels are stored fortunes in gold and banknotes. Never open to the public.

Houses of Parliament Westminster Embankment, SW1. A timeless symbol of free democratic government, to men and women all over the world. It was rebuilt in 1840 on the site of the old Palace of Westminster, which had been destroyed by fire. When Parliament is sitting, a flag flies from the tower by day. Big Ben, the famous 13-ton bell in the 320-foot tower, strikes the hours, and the clock is visible from all over the area. It gets its name from Sir Benjamin Hall, who was Commissioner of Works when the tower was erected in 1859. The square beside it was designed by Sir Charles Barry, to give the best views of the great building, and to act as garden leading to Westminster Abbey across the way. There is a free public gallery, usually open when Parliament is sitting.

Mayfair W1. The grand little neighborhood, roughly half a mile square, that is bounded by Park Lane, Piccadilly, Bond Street, and Oxford Street. Sydney Smith, the 19th-century writer, once said that Mayfair "enclosed more intelligence and ability, to say nothing of wealth and beauty, than the world had ever collected into such a space before." It is still the most prestigious address in London, though very few people live there anymore, and most of the elegant old townhouses are now embassies, offices, or some of the most expensive shops in the world. It is pleasant to stroll past its rows of graceful Georgian houses, with broad mews behind them. In the center of Mayfair is the graceful Grosvenor Square, sadly defaced by the hideous American Embassy building designed by Eero Saarinen. In the square is the Roosevelt Memorial, a statue of FDR built after the Second World War as a symbol of Britain's gratitude. It was financed by public subscription, and it took less than 6 days to raise the money. Two blocks away is Berkeley Square which was once one of London's most aristocratic squares.

Old Bailey Old Bailey Street, EC4. Formally known

Sights

as the Central Criminal Court, this building houses the courtrooms in which some of Britain's worst offenders—ax murderers and such—have been tried. When the court is in session, it is fun to visit the public gallery (entrance around the corner in Newgate). It will remind you of *Witness for the Prosecution*.

Piccadilly Circus W1. London's show business center, this famous circle has gotten pretty tawdry, à la Times Square. But it is still a thrilling sight at night, and if you raise your eyes above street level, the façades facing on the circus form a beautiful unit. A recently opened shopping complex called 'Trocadero' is definitely worth a visit. Behind it is Soho, with its good restaurants and theaters but, sadly, now almost dominated by the mood of sex shops.

River Thames Boat Trips See details under CHILDREN'S LONDON

St. Paul's Cathedral EC4. Sir Christopher Wren, the architect of this magnificent church, is buried in its crypt with the famous inscription "*Si Monumentum requiris circumspice*" (If you seek his monument, look around). And quite a monument it is. Wren's masterpiece, with its 2 baroque towers and its stately dome, was the setting in 1981 of Prince Charles's marriage to Lady Diana Spencer, as 700 million television viewers around the world know. The hardy should by all means climb to the top of the dome for a spectacular view of London, stopping on the way at the whispering gallery, which children love. A whisper in front of the wall on one side of the gallery can be heard clearly at a spot directly across the way, 108 feet distant in a straight line. There are also other Wren churches all over this ancient neighborhood.

Trafalgar Square SW1. Laid out as a war memorial and named after the victory of the Trafalgar, the square was completed in 1841. Just to make sure that the French got the idea, the reliefs of battle scenes at the base of the 145-foot Nelson Column that dominates the square were made of bronze that had been cast from captured French cannons. The tourist center of London, always full of pigeons and photographers.

Victoria Embankment The stretch of the north bank of the Thames that runs between Blackfriars Bridge and Westminster Bridge, a very agreeable walk of about a mile and a quarter. Along the way you pass Cleopatra's Needle, a 3,000-year-old Egyptian obelisk

Sights

which once stood in front of the Temple of the Sun at Heliopolis, and was brought to Britain in the late 19th century, the enormously pleasant Victoria Embankment Gardens (see PARKS.), the temple gardens of the legal fraternity, and various boats moored to the side, including a floating restaurant.

Westminster Abbey SW1. The great church and burial ground. An architectural masterpiece, the Abbey has long been used for occasions of state and royal pageantry. Until George II, most of the Kings of England were buried in the Abbey, and almost all have been crowned there as well. It is also a religious place of great solemnity, the essayist Joseph Addison said, "When I am in a serious humor, I very often walk by myself in Westminster Abbey." So can you. The trouble is that it is often so crowded, especially in the summer. So if you can arrange to attend a service in the Abbey, you will get a better feel for the place. Just inside the west door is a memorial to Winston Churchill, who is buried near Blenheim. Straight ahead is the tomb of the Unknown Warrior from the First World War.

Westminster Cathedral SW1. The Roman Catholic counterpart to the Abbey, and just a short walk away. It was built at the turn of the century in a striking Byzantine style, with an exterior of alternate narrow bands of red brick and gray stone. The interior is a very attractive blend of brick, marble, and mosaic. An elevator takes visitors to the top of the 284-foot tower, from which there is a spectacular view. Try to attend a full choral service in the cathedral on some religious occasion such as Christmas Eve. The choir sings from the high altar, a splendid experience.

Landmarks

Albert Memorial Kensington Gardens, just across from Royal Albert Hall. A grand, high victorian symbol of Queen Victoria's love for her lost husband, Albert. Took 20 years to construct.

Blackfriars Bridge EC4. Named after the Black Friars of the 13th-century monastery which was on the north side of the Thames, near where the bridge is now.

Carlyle's House 24 Cheyne Row, SW3. Thomas Carlyle, the writer, lived here from 1834 until his death

KEW GARDENS

in 1881. Very well preserved. Open 11–1, 2:30 to dusk, year round except December, when it is closed for the month.

Chiswick House Burlington Lane, Chiswick. Fine example of palladian architecture, set in delightful gardens, built in the 1720s by Richard Boyle for the third Earl of Burlington. Open daily 9:30–5:30 in the summer and Wednesday–Sunday 9:30–4 P.M. in winter.

Downing Street SW1. A 1-block street famous for the Prime Minister's residence, which is at No. 10. The Chancellor of the Exchequer lives at No. 11. Unfortunately, it has lately been closed to tourists, because of the fear of terrorist bombing. But you can stand at the Whitehall end and watch the famous come and go.

Duke of York's Column Waterloo Place, SW1. Erected in 1833 as a memorial to Frederick, Duke of York, who was the second son of George III, who, according to the old song, led 10,000 men up a hill and then down again.

Fleet Street EC4. The center of British journalism, the term has become generic, like Madison Avenue. Named for the Fleet River, or Fleet Ditch, which flows from Hampstead down to the Thames nearby. Some critics of the press think it appropriate that the Fleet is now a sewer.

Guildhill EC2. Dating from the 15th century, the Guildhall is the center of civic government, and the site of various ceremonies such as the Lord Mayor's procession in November (SEE ANNUAL EVENTS).

Lambeth Palace Lambeth Palace Road, SE1; 928-6222. For 7 centuries, the London residence of the Archbishop of Canterbury. Library contains more than 1,500 manuscripts. Admission by appointment.

Lancaster House Stable Yard (across from Clarence House), a splendid 19th-century palace now used as a conference center. The independence of Zimbabwe was negotiated here in 1979.

Leicester Square WC2. Now tawdry and shabby, Leicester Square has historic interest only. In the 18th century, it was an artists' center, and residence to, among others, Hogarth and Reynolds. The square was famous for its music halls in the early years of the 20th century.

Lombard Street EC3. Now world-renowned as a banking and financial center. Lombard Street takes its name from the Lombard goldsmiths and moneylenders who set up shop here after the expulsion of the Jews in the 13th century.

London Bridge The first bridge on this site was built by the Romans, the present one in 1967–1973.

Mansion House EC4. The official residence of the Lord Mayors of London, it was built in 1753.

Marble Arch Until 1851 it was the entrance to Buckingham Palace, designed by Nash. Now at the northeast corner of Hyde Park.

Monument Near King William Street, EC3. A fluted doric column 202 feet high, erected right after the great fire of 1666. Walk up the 311 steps to the top and you'll get a fantastic view.

Oratory Brompton Road, SW3. The Brompton Oratory, as people call it, is a beautiful Roman Catholic church, built in the 19th century in the Italian renaissance style.

Royal Hospital Royal Hospital Road, SW3. Near the river in a pleasant corner of Chelsea, the Royal Hospital was founded by King Charles II as a home for retired soldiers, and designed by Wren.

Savoy Chapel Savoy Hill, WC2. Built in 1505 on the site of the 13th century Savoy Palace. Site of Savoy conference of 1661 on revision of the prayer book.

Sir John Soane's Museum Lincoln's Inn Fields, WC2. Built in 1812 as home of Sir John Soane, architect, contains his personal museum. Open Tuesday–Saturday, 10–5. Free. Knock hard on the door to get in.

Somerset House Strand, WC2. Originally the palace of the Dukes of Westminster. Present building, office of Population Censuses and Surveys. Built in late 18th century.

Stock Exchange Old Broad Street, EC2. London's stock market center. Open weekdays from 10–3:30.

Temple Bar Strand, WC2. Temple Bar memorial, built in 1880 on the site of the Wren's 17th-century Temple Bar, marks the boundary of the City of London. When the monarch visits this part of London, she (or he) still stops here to get the Lord Mayor's permission to enter.

Tower Bridge E1, near the Tower. Completed in the last decade of the 19th century, it has 2 huge drawbridges which are regularly raised for passing traffic. There is a museum in the tower. Also a public walkway across the top. Times are advertised, but vary.

University of London Russell Square, WC1. Widely scattered about town, but centered here, the University was founded in 1836.

George Washington Statue Trafalgar Square. A bronze copy of Jean Antoine's marble statue at Richmond, Virginia, this one was presented by the state of Virginia in 1921, and stands in front of the National Gallery. When he led the rebellion, Washington might have been amused by the idea.

Waterloo Place Pall Mall, SW1. Overlooking St. James's Park, it contains monuments to Florence Nightingale and Edward VII.

SINGLES CLUBS

Not much of a singles-club scene in London, but the idea is catching on.

Intervarsity Club 2–5 The Piazza, off James Street, WC2; 240-2525. An activities club aimed at the 20- to 35-year-old graduate bracket. Publishes a monthly magazine.

London Leisure 37B Lilyville Road, SW6; 731-4368. Aimed at people 25 to 45, and fairly upper-middle-class. Holds meetings at various hotels in central London.

London Linkup 102 Newgate Street, EC1; 606-1750. Introductory meetings at the International Sportswriters' Club, Great Russell Street, WC1. Mondays and Thursdays, 6:30 and 8.

London Village 731-4366. Same address as London Leisure, which is an upmarket offshoot of it. London Village is big, old, and well established, with a monthly magazine and many organized events. Introductory meetings at the Royal Court Hotel, Sloane Square, SW1, Tuesdays at 6:15 and 8:30, Sundays at 3:30.

Singles Society 23 Abingdon Road, W8; 937-6503. Meetings at the Tiles Wine Bar, 36 Buckingham Palace Road, SW1, Monday 6–8.
Spare Time Club 10A The Mall, W5; 579-7101. Two different age groups: 18–24 and 25–40.

SPORTS AND SPORTING EVENTS

What follows is a quick guide to the big 3 of British spectator sports: cricket, football, and rugby.
Cricket A national mania. For information on amateur leagues, phone the National Cricket Association at 289-1611. For professional play, *Lord's Cricket Ground* must be the most famous in the world, with a season that lasts from April to September. It is in St. John's Wood, NW8; 289-1615. Another famous cricket ground is the *Oval*, south of the river in Kennington, SE11; 582-6660.
Football The game that the Americans call soccer is by far the most popular British sport, both for spectators and for amateur leagues. To every little boy in the country, it is what baseball is to Americans. Professionally, the English Football League has 92 clubs, divided into four divisions. They play every Saturday afternoon at 3 and sometimes during the week in the evening from August to April, when the F.A. (Football Association) and Milk Cup finals are held at Wembley, in London. The F.A. Cup is played on the first Saturday in May.
Rugby Headquarters for this game, which is somewhat similar to American football, is the Rugby Football Union, Whitton Road, Twickenham, Middlesex. Phone 892-8161 for details and schedules.

Amateur Athletic Organizations

Amateur Athletics Association Francis House, Francis Street, SW1; 828-8379. Supplies lists of clubs and a diary of events.

British Canoeing Union Flexel House, 45–47 High Street, Addlestone, Surrey. Phone Weybridge 41341 for information and advice about canoeing on the Thames and other nearby rivers.

British Cycling Federation 16 Upper Woburn Place, WC1; 387-9320. Call for suggestions about cycling trips.

British Hang Gliding Association Corston, Monksilver, Taunton, Somerset. Write for information on hang gliding.

British Parachuting Association Kimberly House, 47 Vaughan Way, Leicester. Phone Leicester 59778 for information and a list of clubs near London (or anywhere in the country).

Croquet Association Hurlingham Club, Ranelagh Gardens, SW6; 736-3148. Call for information and advice.

London Anglers' Association 183 Hoe Street, E17; 520-7477. For information and advice on fishing in London's many waterways. Associate membership is available.

Ski Club of Great Britain 118 Eaton Square, SW1; 235-4711. Grass skiing, from April to October.

Squash Racquets Association 70 Brompton Road, SW3; 828-3064. Publishes a guide to the many courts in London. One of the best is Wembley Squash Courts, Empire Way, Wembley; 902-9230. No membership necessary.

Sports Centers and Gyms

Crystal Palace National Sports Center Crystal Palace, SE19; 778-0131. This is Britain's largest multi-purpose sporting center, with excellent facilities for several dozen different sports. There is a floodlit stadium that seats 15,000, an olympic-size swimming pool, a diving pool, and an indoor sports hall featuring basketball, squash, and other racquet games.

Eastway Cycle Circuit Temple Mills Lane, E15; 534-6085. An enclosed bicycle circuit, with facilities for riding, racing, training, and coaching.

Queen Mother Sports Center Vauxhall Bridge Road (behind Victoria Station). An excellent new complex with a swimming pool, a diving pool, and a wading pool for very small children, plus Ping Pong, basketball, badminton, a bar, and a restaurant.
Sobel Sports Center Hornsey Road, N7; 607-1632. Large indoor center, with courses in gymnastics, hockey, netball, archery, Ping Pong, boxing, and other sports. Also an ice rink, ski slope, and sauna.
Swiss Cottage Sports Center Winchester Road, NW3; 586-5989. Indoor facilities for badminton, basketball, gymnastics, martial arts, squash, and swimming.
YMCA 112 Great Russell Street, WC1; 637-8131. Indoor facilities for badminton, basketball, gymnastics, martial arts, swimming, volleyball, and yoga. Membership necessary.

For Golfers

The *Golf Course Guide*, published by the Daily Telegraph, is a useful reference book for the traveler who wants to play. Also check the *Golfer's Handbook*, which is available in many libraries. Here are some municipal courses, for which you do not need any membership:
Addington Court Featherbed Lane, Addington, Croydon, Surrey; 657-0281. Two 18-hole courses and a 9-hole course.
Beckenham Place Park Beckenham, Kent; 650-2292. 18 holes.
Coulsdon Court Coulsdon, Surrey; 660-0468. 18 holes.
Hainault Forest Chigwell Roy, Hainault, Essex; 500-2470. Two 18-hole courses.
Home Park Hampton Wick, Kingston-upon-Thames, Surrey; 977-6645. 18 holes.
Picketts Lock Centre Picketts Lock Lane, N9; 803-4756. 9 holes.
Royal Epping Forest Forest Approach, Station Road, Chingford, Essex; 529-1039. 18 holes.

For Swimmers

Though it seldom seems warm enough for it, there are several parks that have outdoor swimming in ponds or pools. They are usually open from 7 A.M.–7 P.M.

May–September, 7:30 A.M.–10 A.M. October–April. Free before 9 A.M. But it is best to check first. Here is a listing:
Eltham Park South Baths, SE9; 850-9890.
Fulham Baths, Norman Park, Lillie Road, SW6; 381-4498.
Hampstead Pond, NW3; 435-2366. Free.
Highgate Ponds, N6; 340-4044. Men only. Free
Kenwood Pond, N6; 340-1033. Women only. Free
London Fields Baths, E8; 254-7494.
Parliament Hill Lido, NW5; 485-3873.
Peckham Rye Park Baths, SE22; 732-8157.
Serpentine, Hyde Park, W2; 262-5484.
Southwark Park Baths, SE16; 237-6572.
Tooting Common Baths, SW17; 769-4226.
Victoria Park Lido, E9; 985-6774.

SUBWAY (THE TUBE)
See TRANSPORTATION

TAXIS
See TRANSPORTATION

TEA
See COFFEE AND TEA

TELEPHONES
See INFORMATION

Sports

THEATER

The London stage is one of Britain's major attractions. You can find every imaginable kind of show from the high classical to the radical fringe, and it is usually not much trouble to get a seat, even at the last minute. Here are 2 lists: The major theaters in the West End first, and then "the Fringe," which means anything anywhere else, a term comparable to "off Broadway." Half-price tickets are on sale for that day's shows at an outdoor kiosk in Leicester Square. Check newspapers for times.

Adelphi Strand, WC2; 836-7611. Big musicals and revues.

Albery St. Martin's Lane, WC2; 836-3878. Plays and musicals.

Aldwych 49 Aldwych, WC2; 836-6404. The home of the famous Royal Shakespeare Company.

Ambassadors West Street, Cambridge Circus, WC2; 836-1171. A rather small, intimate theater, this is where Agatha Christie's classic, *The Mousetrap* played for more than 20 years.

Apollo Shaftesbury Avenue, W1; 437-2663. Musical comedy and drama.

Apollo Victoria 17 Wilton Road, SW1; 828-8665. Big musicals.

Astoria 157 Charing Cross Road, WC2; 437-1801. A converted movie theater. Popular musicals.

Barbican Barbican Centre, Barbican, EC2; 628-8795. Definitely worth a visit for the building alone. Royal Shakespeare Company and works of new British playwrights.

Cambridge Earlham Street, WC2; 836-6056. Musicals and plays.

Comedy Panton Street, SW1; 930-2578. Small theater with unusual comedies and small-cast dramas.

Criterion Piccadilly Circus, W1; 930-3216. Small, comfortable, beautiful theater.

Drury Lane Catherine Street, WC2; 836-8108. Opened in 17th century, the famous old Drury Lane has been burned and rebuilt and torn down and rebuilt over the years. A huge old place, suitable for musicals.

Duchess Catherine Street, WC2; 836-8243.

Duke of York's St. Martin's Lane, WC2; 836-5122.
Fortune Russell Street, WC2; 836-2238. Small and intimate.
Garrick Charing Cross Road, WC2; 836-4601. Built at the turn of the century.
Globe Shaftesbury Avenue, W1; 437-1592. Historic old name, the most recent of a number of Globes in London. Musicals.
Haymarket (Theatre Royal) Haymarket, SW1; 930-9832. Built by Nash in the early 19th century. Plays.
Her Majesty's Haymarket, SW1; 930-6606. Musicals and plays.
Lyric Shaftesbury Avenue, W1; 437-3686. Oldest theater in Shaftesbury, the Lyric was built in the 1880s.
Mayfair Stratton Street, W1; 629-3036. In the Mayfair hotel.
Mermaid Puddle Dock, Blackfriars, EC4; 236-5568. Plays and musicals, with a restaurant and two bars overlooking the Thames.
National South Bank, SE1; 928-2252. Opened in 1976 as part of the South Bank arts center, the National is actually 3 theaters: the Olivier, the Lyttleton, and the Cottesloe. The home of the renowned National Theatre Company.
New London Drury Lane, WC2; 405-0072. Opened in 1972.
Old Vic Waterloo Road, SE1; 928-7616. Built in the early 19th century, the famous Old Vic was the home of the National Theatre until it moved into the South Bank. Its Shakespeare and other classic works are still often outstanding.
Palace Cambridge Circus, WC2; 437-6834. Originally an opera house, now stages big musicals.
Palladium 8 Argyll Street, W1; 437-7373. Houses variety shows and musicals.
Phoenix Charing Cross Road, WC2; 836-8611.
Piccadilly Denman Street, W1; 437-4506.
Prince Edward Old Compton Street, W1; 437-6877. Formerly a caberet, and then a cinema, it now stages hit musicals.
Prince of Wales Coventry Street, W1; 930-8681.
Queen's Shaftesbury Avenue, W1; 734-1166. Bombed out during the Second World War, and reopened only in 1959.

10 DOWNING STREET

Royal Court Sloane Square, SW1; 730-1745. Hope of the English Stage Company. Very good productions, including experimental.
Royal Shakespeare Company. See under BARBICAN.
Royalty Portugal Street, WC2; 405-8004.
St. Martin's West Street, Cambridge Circus, WC2; 836-1443. Small, intimate playhouse.
Savoy Strand, WC2; 836-8888. Plays, comedies, and musicals. The first theater in London to be fully lit by electricity.
Shaftesbury Shaftesbury Avenue, WC2; 836-6596. Musicals.
Strand Strand, WC2; 836-2660.
Vaudeville Strand, WC2; 836-9988. Originally specialized in vaudeville, then converted to stage plays.
Westminster Palace Street, Buckingham Palace Road, SW1; 834-0283.
Whitehall (Theater of War, World War II Museum) 14 Whitehall, SW1; 930-7765.
Wyndham's Charing Cross, WC2; 836-3028. Small, lovely theater founded by Sir Charles Wyndham.

Fringe

Albany Empire Douglas Way, Deptford, SE8; 691-3333. Avant-garde plays.
Arts Theater Club 6–7 Great Newport Street, WC2; 836-2132. Old and new plays.
Cockpit Theater Gateforth Street, NW8; 402-5081. Theater-in-the-round with drama and experimental productions.
Gate at The Latchmere 503 Battersea Park Road, SW11; 228-2620. Theater above a pub.
Half Moon 213 Mile End Road, E1; 790-4000. Political, experimental plays, many of them about East London and its problems.
Hampstead Theater Club Swiss Cottage Centre, Avenue Road, NW3; 722-9301. New drama and revivals.
Institute of Contemporary Arts (ICA) Nash House, The Mall, SW1; 930-3647. Contemporary drama with restaurant. Buckingham Palace is at the other end of The Mall.
Jeanetta Cochrane Theater Southhampton Row, WC1; 242-7040. Theater of the Central School of Art and Design. Experimental shows and new drama.

Lyric Hammersmith King Street, W6; 741-2311. Historic building, carefully restored. Its Studio Theater has cabaret and experimental shows.
New End 27 New End, NW3; 435-6053. New plays, experimental productions.
Oval House 54 Kennington Oval, SE11; 735-2786. Two experimental theaters.
Players Hungerford Arches, Villiers Street, WC2; 839-1134. A relic of the Victorian music hall tradition, with good and lively shows. Join in the singing. Membership must be obtained 48 hours in advance.
Riverside Studios Crisp Road, W6; 748-3354. Various music and dance programs.
Shaw Theater 100 Euston Road, NW1; 388-1394. Especially interesting for young people and students.
Theater Royal Gerry Raffles Square, E15; 534-0310. New plays and musicals.
Theater Upstairs Royal Court Theater, Sloane Square, SW1; 730-2554. A small, intimate room above the regular theater, showing new plays.
Vanbrugh 62 Gower Street, WC1; 580-7982. Two theaters showing experimental productions and revivals by students at the Royal Academy of Dramatic Art (RADA).
Warehouse Donmar Theater, 41 Earlham Street, WC2; 836-6808. Evening and late night entertainment.
Young Vic 66 The Cut, Waterloo, SE1; 928-6363. Interesting new productions of Shakespeare, and experimental theater.

TOILETRIES
See PERFUMES AND TOILETRIES

TOURS AND SIGHTSEEING

For starters, the best and cheapest way to hit the high spots is in the Round London Sightseeing Tour run by London Transport (the bus and underground authority). The 20-mile circuit takes 2 hours and covers all the most famous landmarks in Central London. You can board it at any of 3 stops along the route: Piccadilly Circus, Victoria, or Marble Arch. It runs at least every hour from 9–4, no reservations needed. The price is about £4–£5. The disadvantage of this tour is that there is no guide, but they do give you a useful map of the route as you board.

Once you know your way around a bit, the best buy for getting around is a Go As you Please ticket on London Transport, which gives you unlimited travel for a period of 3 days, 4 days, or a week, at a substantial saving, or obtain a weekly pass at any tube station (one passport size photo required).

If you want a guided tour, London Transport provides them too, covering the same route for £4, or longer tours for more money. They should be booked at any of the London Transport Travel Information Centers (for locations see INFORMATION). There are also a number of private tour operators, including the following:

American Express 6 Haymarket, SW1; 930-4411.
Evan Evans 25A Cockspur Street, SW1; 930-2377.
Frames 11 Herbrand Street, WC1; 837-3111.
Thomas Cook 45 Berkeley Street, W1; 499-4000.

Information is also available from the British Tourist Authority at 64 St. James's Street, SW1; 629-9191. This B.T.A. office, as noted elsewhere in this guide, is very well staffed, well informed, and friendly, and if they do not know the answer to the tourist's question, they are likely to know who does.

You can also get a wealth of good guided tours on foot in London, exploring every aspect of the city's history and culture. There is a walking tour of Jack the Ripper's London, a pub walk, a walk through the 1666 fire and the Great Plague, and many others. Details

and programs available from the B.T.A. office in St. James's (see above) or from either of two operators:
Guided Walks 11 Pennyfields, Warley, Brentwood, Essex; (0277) 213704.
London Walks 139 Conway Road, London N14; 882-2763.

Walking on your own in London is also one of the city's great attractions. Because the city is so old, its streets twist and turn along ancient paths, and there is always something interesting around the corner. One that particularly appeals is from St. Paul's Cathedral to Parliament, along the north bank of the Thames, which is known as Victoria Embankment. You pass ships and parks, and as you walk the skyline changes around you; it's a good walk for a clear, cold night. Almost any walk in Mayfair is also delightful, imagining the high life of London's rich, especially in the years between the wars.

TOYS

Most department stores have extensive toy departments. And in this category, as in so many others, Harrods is Number One, with Hamleys a close second. Here are some shops that specialize in toys:
Dolls' House 116 Lisson Grove, NW1; 723-1418. A wide variety of dolls' houses and furniture for them. Many antiques.
Dolls' Hospital 16 Dawes Road, SW6; 385-2081. Apart from repairing them, they also have dolls and toys for sale.
Hamleys 188–196 Regent Street, W1; 734-3161. Quite the most wonderful toy store in London. Has some of everything, for all ages. Even the grown-ups could be tempted.
James Galt 30 Great Marlborough Street, W1; 734-0829. Well-designed toys for under-9s. Also some children's furnishings and wall hangings.
Kristin Baybars 3 Mansfield Road, NW5; 267-0934. Specializes in handmade and little tiny toys. Also dolls' houses.

Pollock's Toy Shop 1 Scala Street, WC1. 636-3452. Old-fashioned and modern toys, and cut-out Victorian model theaters.

Tiger, Tiger 219 King's Road, SW3; 352-8080. Well known for its stunning window displays. Craftsmen-made toys, and anything from 3 pence to 200 pence!

Tree House 237 Kensington High Street, W8; 937-7497. A wide variety of toys of all kinds. They also have a soda fountain selling ice cream, milkshakes, toasted sandwiches, croissants and iced coffee, among other goodies.

TRANSPORTATION

London has very good public transportation—buses and the underground (also called the "tube," but not the "subway," which means simply a pedestrian tunnel). But the system virtually closes down at midnight, which can be a great inconvenience. Underground stations have signs telling the schedule of the last trains (and the first in the early morning). There is a limited network of "night buses," which operates all night, but infrequently. They are the same red, double-decker buses, but the route is identified by the letter N; Route 97, for example, becomes N97.

The city's familiar black taxis are a joy, though sometimes difficult to find late at night, particularly if you need one just after the underground system has closed. The fare structure includes a bewildering array of surcharges—for luggage, for evening, for weekend, for Christmas, for extra passengers—all explained on a plaque displayed in front of the passenger. The drivers have all spent a year learning the city, so they rarely have to ask directions.

When Londoners say British Rail, they mean suburban and long-distance trains, which come in and out of London at various so-called main-line stations situated in a circle around the center of town. The British Rail system connects well to the underground system; there is a major underground station at each of the British Rail terminals. But the 2 are separate, with separate fare structures.

Getting in from Heathrow on the underground is particularly easy, unless you have a great deal of luggage. The Piccadilly line station is right in the airport, linked by tunnels to all 3 terminals. That will take you through South Kensington to Piccadilly Circus, and beyond, with all sorts of transfer points along the way. Depending on the time of day, it takes 40 or 50 minutes to get to central London. Getting in from Gatwick is a bit more complicated. You take the British Rail train (leaving every 15 minutes or so) on a 40-minute trip to Victoria Station, and link up with bus, taxi or underground there.

TUBE

See TRANSPORTATION

WEATHER

London weather is much maligned. Sure, it rains a lot, but not all the time. And the proper Englishman's umbrella is intended to do much more for him and his image than just keep the rain away. The old pea-soup fogs of Dickens's and Jack the Ripper's day almost never occur any more, thanks to stricter air pollution control laws. Americans should remember that London never gets anything like as cold or as hot as most parts of the United States. The temperature is rarely below 32 degrees on the very coldest days in winter, and on the rare summer days when it gets up into the upper 70s or lower 80s, they talk of "a scorcher." British homes are therefore almost never air conditioned. But by the same token, many of them are not very well heated (and there are still many Britons who simply do not have central heating at all). Thus, in winter it is wise to dress warmly when visiting a British home, perhaps in layers that you can peel off if it is warmer than expected.

WINE BARS

The wine bar, a delightful London institution, is rather less formal than most restaurants, with rather better food than most pubs. Generally open regular pub hours. Here are a few favorites:

Bill Bentley's 31 Beauchamp Place, SW3; 589-5080. Well known for its seafood, especially oysters. In a good shopping neighborhood.
Brays Wine Bar 198 Fulham Road, SW10; 352-0251. A pleasant and relaxed place with good food.
Corkscrew 77 Dorothy Road, SW11; 228-1311. Relaxing decor, serves Viennese food at reasonable prices, with background classical music. Small parties catered for.
Draycott's 114 Draycott Avenue, SW3; 584-5359. Very stylish place where the best-seller is champagne. Good pâtés, mousses, and game pies.
Ebury 139 Ebury Street, SW1; 730-5447. Good salads, other cold dishes. The Ebury is long established and very popular.
El Vino 47 Fleet Street, EC4; 353-6786. Very popular with journalists and the lawyers in the neighborhood, especially at lunchtime.
Fino's Cellar 104 Charing Cross Road, WC2; 836-1077. A good place for a bite before or after the theater.

Julie's Bar 137 Portland Road, W11; 727-7985. Very popular place with armchairs and good fresh fish.

Loose Box 136 Brompton Road, SW1; 584-9280. If you are exhausted after shopping at Harrods, this will help to relax you. Restaurant upstairs, and lively in the evenings.

Motcomb's 26 Motcomb Street, SW1; 235-6382. A very stylish and elegant place, in snappy Belgravia. Excellent assortment of cheeses.

Russkies Wine Cellar 6 Wellington Terrace, Bayswater, W2; 229-9128. A pleasant friendly place with good cold food and a daily casserole or stew.

Saucy Grape 73 Wigmore Street, W1; 486-3551. A bright busy place with jukebox music and a friendly bustle. Pianists/singers.

Shampers 4 Kingly Street, W1; Close to Liberty's. Delicious cold buffet. Candlelight and taped jazz.

Whittington's 21 College Hill, EC4; 248-5855. A picturesque wine vault, or cellar, with good cheese and salads. Open at lunchtime and early evening.

WINES AND LIQUORS

Alcoholic beverages are generally very expensive in Britain, because of taxes. Even a bottle of Scotch costs much more in Scotland, and in London, than in many parts of the United States and Europe. Prices vary considerably, so it is wise to shop around. Here are a couple of stores to delight any shopper.

Berry Brothers & Rudd 3 St. James's Street, SW1; 930-1888. A splendid old store in a house that was built in 1730 and looks as if it hasn't changed since. Superb port and excellent claret, and a wide range of conventional liquors. But the place is well worth a visit even if you don't want to buy anything. They have the old scale on which gentlemen used to weigh themselves (back in the days before bathroom scales), and a 19th-century register of who weighed what.

Christie's 8 King Street, SW1; 839-9060. Wine auctions usually held on Thursdays.

Corney and Barrow 12 Helmet Row, EC1; 251-4051. A reputation for the very best in vintage port and claret.

Harveys of Bristol 27 Pall Mall, SW1; 839-4691. Highly reputable group offering an excellent list.

O. W. Loeb & Co. 15 Jermyn Street, SW1; 734-5878. Said to have the most complete list of German wines in the country, a major importer of Moselles. This is not a shop. You write or phone your order.

Oddbins 41 Farringdon Street, EC4; 236-7721. Many other branches around town. Palatable plonk (cheapish) or other more expensive wines. A huge selection usually.

Soho Wine Market 3 Greek Street, W1; 437-9311. The largest selection of single malt Scotch whiskies in London. Over a hundred different brands, at the last count. Run by two cheerful Scottish brothers named Milroy.

ZOOS

See CHILDREN'S LONDON

MAPS

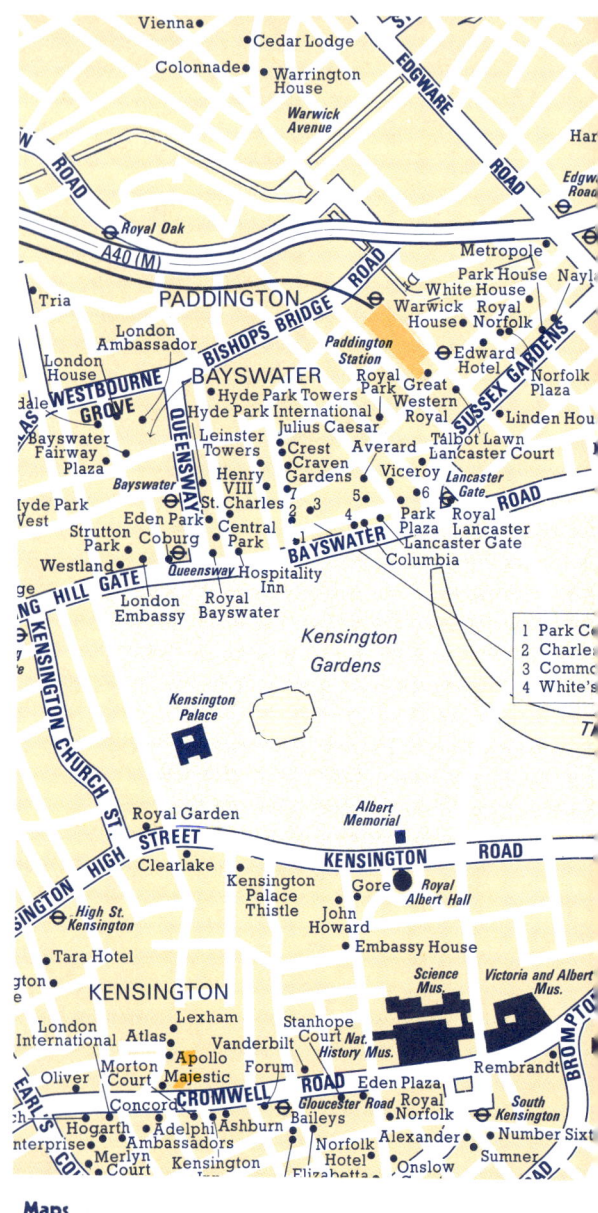

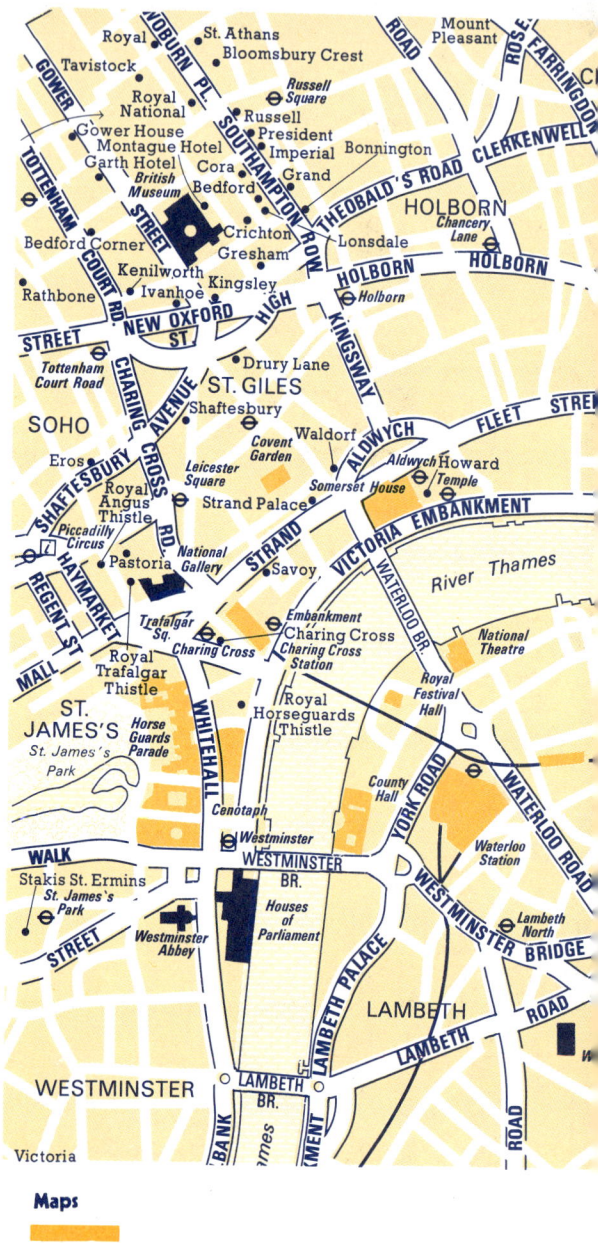

Maps

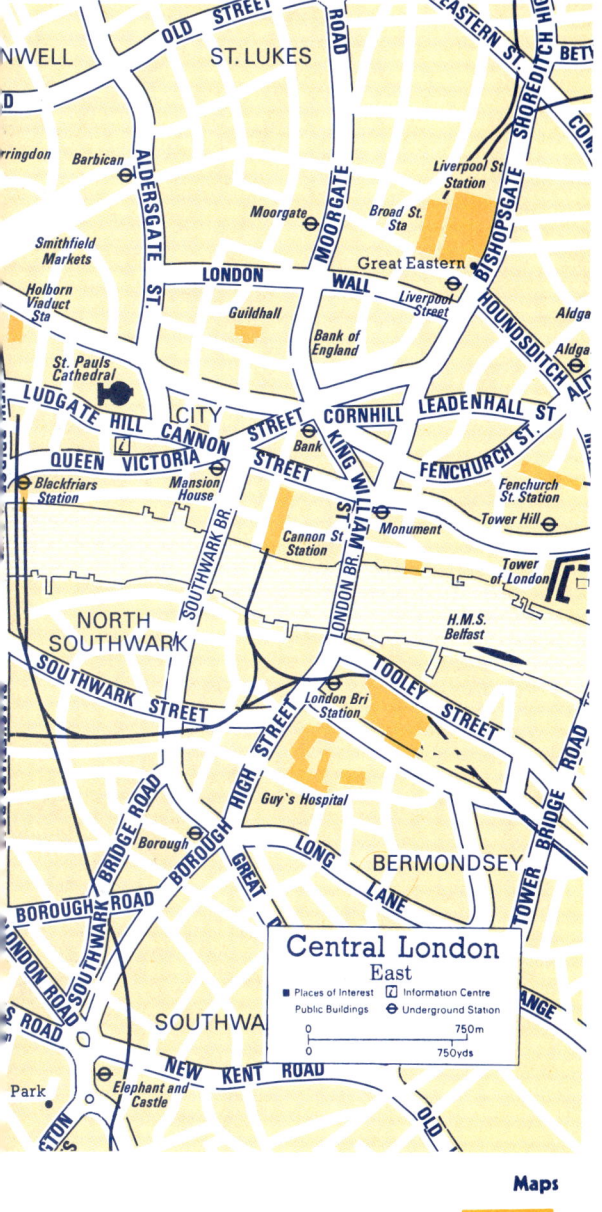

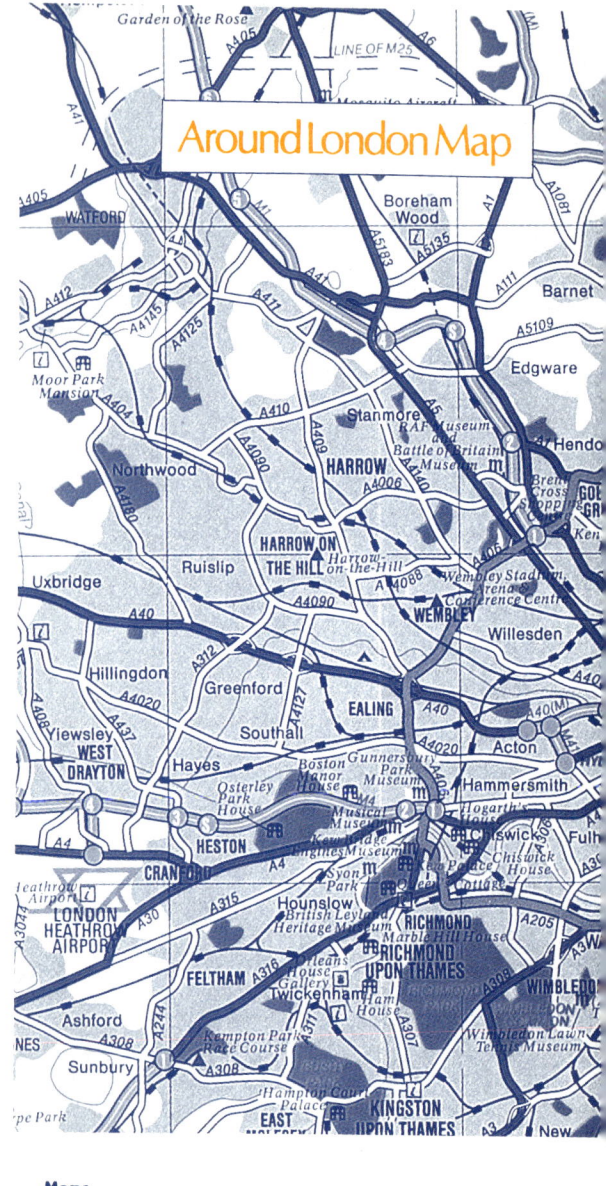

Maps

TIPS FOR TAKING THE UNDERGROUND

Travel on London's Underground is simple. The routes are extensive, allowing you to travel about the city quickly.

* There are various special transport tickets available to tourists. The most popular (and best for the money) is the "Go-As-You-Please" ticket. It gives you 3, 4, or 7 days of unlimited travel on London's red buses and on the Underground. You can buy tickets at most London Transport Underground stations or at Travel Information Centers. Other specials are: the Central Tube Red Rover and the Red Bus Rover. Travel Information Centers can help you with these as well.

* Travel Information Centers are open 7 days a week, form 8:30 AM to 9:30 PM at: Victoria, Piccadilly Circus, Charing Cross, King's Cross, Oxford Circus, St. James's Park, Euston, Heathrow Central Underground stations and at Waterloo British Rail Travel Center.

* The Underground goes almost everywhere, but remember that trains do not run all night and some stations are closed on weekends. If you plan to be out late, check what time the last train leaves.

* It's easy to get to and from the airports on the Underground. For Heathrow take the Piccadilly Line; for Gatwick take British Rail's Rapid City Link from Victoria.

* Fares vary according to the distance traveled, so be sure to consult the list of fares posted in each station. You buy your ticket (either from an agent of from a machine) before traveling. Then either show it to the collector or, for the automated stations, put it through the automatic entry gate and walk through. Remember to pick up your ticket as you pass through the gate, and keep it with you till the end of your trip. You may be asked to show or surrender it, and there are stiff fines and heavy penalties for people who cheat the system.